What people

Polytheism: A [

"Steven Dillon's book is a major contribution to the polytheist revival, taking on the big questions about the Gods and the world in a way that will be useful to polytheists in any tradition, or to seekers just trying to understand a polytheistic worldview. Dillon draws upon major currents of the Western philosophical tradition without requiring any prior familiarity with these. Through his careful, step-by-step arguments, the reader will come to see the rational basis for devotion to the Gods."
Edward P. Butler, PhD, Director, Center for Global Polytheist and Indigenous Traditions, Indic Academy

"Steven Dillon's *Polytheism: A Platonic Approach* provides a great starting point for anyone who is looking to explore the philosophy behind polytheism. It provides an overview of the arguments of polytheism in a way which doesn't try to convince the reader of their merit, but instead simply presents the arguments as they are. With a clear and well-defined structure, the concepts within this book are easy for even the novice to follow. This is a great book for all those looking to gain more of a big-picture view of the philosophy behind polytheism."
Jessica Howard, author of *The Art of Lithomancy*

"This short book is a very interesting exposition and defence of a polycentric Platonic theism (of something like the kind defended by Proclus, Plotinus and Iamblichus). Many readers will be struck by similarities between familiar kinds of Thomism and the view defended in this book. Polycentric Platonic theism embraces, for example, divine transcendence, divine ineffability, divine otherness and divine simplicity."
Graham Oppy, Professor of Philosophy, Monash University

Pagan Portals
Polytheism:
A Platonic Approach

Pagan Portals
Polytheism:
A Platonic Approach

Steven Dillon

**MOON
BOOKS**

Winchester, UK
Washington, USA

JOHN HUNT PUBLISHING

First published by Moon Books, 2022
Moon Books is an imprint of John Hunt Publishing Ltd., No. 3 East Street, Alresford
Hampshire SO24 9EE, UK
office@jhpbooks.net
www.johnhuntpublishing.com
www.moon-books.net

For distributor details and how to order please visit the 'Ordering' section on our website.

ISBN: 978 1 78535 979 8
978 1 78535 980 4 (ebook)
Library of Congress Control Number: 2021942757

A CIP catalogue record for this book is available from the British Library.

Design: Matthew Greenfield

UK: Printed and bound by CPI Group (UK) Ltd, Croydon, CR0 4YY
Printed in North America by CPI GPS partners

We operate a distinctive and ethical publishing philosophy in
all areas of our business, from our global network of authors to
production and worldwide distribution.

Contents

Previous Titles

The Case for Polytheism
978-1-78279-735-7 (Paperback)
978-1-78279-734-0 (ebook)

To reaching for what's beyond your grasp.
This one's for you Lune.

Acknowledgments

Edward Butler introduced me to the idea of polycentricity and its conceptual repertoire, he gave me a new vocabulary and showed me many of its applications. His challenging works, invaluable feedback, editorial comments, and cherished friendship helped bring to life the synthesis of thought between these pages. Thank you, Edward, for everything. But there are others to blame for this, such as my wife. She is preeminently guilty of encouraging me to think and write and of inspiring me to live the good life. And if that is not bad enough, she manages to make that look easy; graceful as always. Then there are those in the polytheist community who enabled my philosophical lifestyle, in one way or another. Look what you did. Finally, there are also those with whom I deployed, during which time so much of this was written. Thank you. There is a reason I was so creative and productive during that time, and that is you.

Introduction

This is the sort of book that I wish had been around when I first began looking into polytheism: a pithy and informal presentation of the *gist* of a polytheist worldview; what it all looks like in the big picture: the Gods, the world and us. Not a presentation of its history or the practices and beliefs of this or that polytheist religion, though such works are obviously paramount, but of the *idea* of polytheism itself and what it implies about everything else. What are the Gods and where do they fit into the picture? What is a world with Gods supposed to look like and what would it mean for us? Presenting this idea and reflecting on it by giving one a feel for the spirit of polytheism is a markedly different approach to such matters than what one may find in today's more apologetically driven works on the philosophy of religion; namely, the stitching together of loosely related arguments into a cumulative case that inconclusively favors a more abstract position of which the God or religion that one wishes to argue on behalf is but an instance.

Short and sweet, the sort of approach I have in mind would give the reader the information she needs without dragging her down rabbit holes or drowning her in detail. Relaxed, its style would present this information in as digestible a manner as possible. Holistic, this style would show the reader what the image on the box looks like *before* she digs through all the puzzle pieces, rather than trying to figure out what that image is *from* the pieces that happen to have been looked at so far. For all these good intentions, there will be deep discussions and unfamiliar terms in what follows; it just comes with the territory. But I hope I can spare the reader some of the time and energy she would otherwise have spent. And if after reading this she wishes to pursue polytheism in greater depths, there is only an abundance of sources to which she could turn. Indeed, Platonism is in some ways a Theory of Everything.

This work stands in stark contrast to my earlier monograph *The Case for Polytheism*. In the years that followed its publication, I came to discover that what I had been looking for all along without knowing it was the organic, bottomless and intricately interwoven polytheist picture of reality that coursed through the veins of ancient Platonism. It made polytheism even more enchanting, and my personal philosophy began to reflect the content of what I became enamored with. In light of this, the reader will find that in contrast to *The Case*, no probabilistic considerations will be offered here; no inferences to the best explanation will be given, nor any costs-benefits analyses provided. Although these analytic methods and others like them have their place, it is not here. I had hoped in *The Case* that folks would mount further cases for polytheism based on their own schools of thought. This work may be considered to do just this from a Platonic perspective.

As one will have already gathered, this is more of an exhibit than an introduction. It is not a disinterested listing of facts and descriptions about a position that one observes or evaluates from the outside, but the putting on display of a view of all things as they seem to be. No apologies will be made for this and I mention it only as fair warning to those who might appreciate an early head's up. Despite the nature of this material, it is not a work of apologetics in the typical sense: it is an attempt to show one what theism really amounts to, not necessarily to convince her that theism is true. In this way, readers from any background can appreciate the material without it needlessly triggering any predispositions in them to be more critical of it than they may otherwise have been. However, for those who would like to see what could be said on its behalf, appendixes are included at the end that address crucial parts of the system here presented.

The general methodology of this work is to reason from the Gods rather than to them. In other words, the Gods are like a first principle or axiom from which a system follows. In this top-down approach we will develop a feel for what theism amounts to and allow it to unfold for itself the picture of reality that it implies or predicts. Chapter 1 will kick this process off by introducing theism as a view on which there is more to reality than Nature. As we shall see, to transcend Nature is to be ineffable, and through implication, entailment and prediction, the inner logic of ineffability, will bloom into an entire polytheist worldview. This will become readily apparent in Chapter 2 where the notions from the preceding chapter are taken to their logical conclusions, and it is shown that theism just is polytheism. Chapter 3 will, in turn, take the notion of polytheism to its logical conclusions and find that all things relate to the Gods through emanation and constitution. Finally, Chapter 4 will close the main body of this work by pursuing what this worldview means for humankind.

Aristotle said it was a divinely inspired "tradition handed down from the ancients of the earliest times" that the Gods, who encompass "the whole of nature" are "the primary substances," (Metaphysics 1074b1-10). What follows is an attempt to honor this most ancient of traditions by sharing with new generations these two grand maxims, namely, that the Gods encompass the whole of nature and that they are the primary substances. Whether polytheist or not, I hope this work helps to enchant the reader as much as Platonism has me.

Steven Dillon,
2020

Chapter 1

Theism

1. To be divine is to transcend Nature.
2. To transcend Nature is to be henadic.
3. To be henadic is to be polycentric.
4. Therefore, to be divine is to be polycentric.

We are going to try to answer a few questions throughout this work. First, what does theism amount to? In other words, what does theism say, involve or imply? In this vein we shall try to get a feel for what divinity *looks* like according to theism: is it singular or plural, transcendent or immanent, personal or mechanical and so on and so forth. We shall attempt to gather this information not by surveying polls, testimonies or literature; but, upon finding a starting point, by analyzing the propositional content of theism itself. In this regard, the nature of our inquiry is philosophical rather than sociological or historical. Our second question will concern what it should all look like, in the big picture, if the theist is correct. In other words, given a sufficiently clear understanding of divinity, what is its overall story and how does it fit in with everything else? While there is overlap between the two questions, they allow us to cover issues that we need to think carefully about from different angles. If after all has been said these questions have been answered in a useful way, this work will have served its purpose. I hope the reader finds what follows to be inspiring, novel and thought-provoking.

A word about the structure and style of the chapters and sections to follow. For the sake of organizing our reflections on these questions and giving them order and direction, the results of each section have been condensed and sewn together

4

into the above argument so that whichever proposition is emboldened at the outset will serve to thematically guide the ensuing discussions as well as to summarize their most crucial content at the end. The overarching argument of this work is thus not included to be a tool of persuasion, though it may be used for that, but to be a tool of presentation and organization. We will begin to use this style here in Chapter 1 by looking at our two basic questions in the context of a discussion about what theism amounts to. This discussion will lead us to affirm the first premise in the above argument: to be divine is to transcend Nature. But, and for future format, before getting into it we shall try and sum up the gist of the discussion to follow.

The Gist: However Nature is to be understood – whether as physical, concrete or causal and so forth – and whatever types of things are thereby to be included within it – the physical, the mental, the moral or the abstract and so forth – theism does not allow that it is *all* there is to reality. But what is theism really saying in this regard? Using science as a guide to what sorts of things count as natural or not, we come to understand that whatever else may be said of Nature it is at least sensible and intelligible, so that according to theism reality is not *just* sensible and intelligible but also ineffable. However, to be ineffable is for one to be so utterly individual that there is nothing more to her than herself to be described as: she has no properties, features or characteristics that are not just herself. Theism thus amounts to a view on which there is someone who is utterly unique because she is beyond Nature.

Section 1.1: Transcending Nature
All that is divine is itself ineffable and unknowable by any secondary being because of its supra-existential unity...
– Proclus, *Elements of* Theology, Proposition 123 (Prop.)

Our work is primarily intended to present in as pithy a manner as feasible a Platonic theism in broad, digestible contours. We are not so much concerned with convincing the reader that this system is *true*. Ironically, it is perhaps by withdrawing from a rhetorical tone that this work will be more beneficial for the unfamiliar reader who wants to be convinced of polytheism because the system itself will not carry with its first impression the strengths or weaknesses of one, particular set of arguments. Instead, the system will be allowed to ruminate in the mind of the reader, inviting and resisting criticisms on its own terms.

However, in line with a more expository approach, we shall take for granted a notion of theism that fits well with this Platonic system; namely, the view that there is more to reality than Nature; that there is something which in fact transcends Nature. For those who are interested in seeing an evaluation of this notion, arguments have been provided in Appendix A. Indeed, for those who may wish to see this system evaluated in general, each appendix provides an argument that covers a crucial point in the overall presentation. For its part, the notion of theism as a view on which there is more to reality than Nature strikes me as straightforwardly commonsensical and as fair a starting point as any. Be that as it may, we shall proceed by taking this notion for granted so that we may expound upon the system itself. To begin then, let us consider what it is to be natural and so what it is that Gods would transcend.

The number of scientific fields that there could in principle be will depend on how many types of things there are in Nature, which of course could be divided up in different ways – e.g. the sub-atomic, the chemical or the biological and so on and so forth. Nature includes the sorts of things that science can study. But one might worry about this general way of putting things because what if it turns out that future science veers far from what current science accepts there to be, so that what Nature is thought to include now differs radically from what Nature will be thought to include in the future? If this were a likely scenario, it would be rather fruitless to think of Nature as being made up of the sorts of things that science can study because what Nature is thought to be made up of will differ from one period of time to the next. But we need not worry about how deeply future science will disagree with current science in what it accepts Nature to be made up of because what matters more is what sorts of things *ideal* science would recognize as natural. Ideal science is a science that is apprised of *all* the relevant facts about Nature as well as the best methods to understand them. Following Oppy's lead (2018), we can say that inasmuch as current science is an attempt to approximate ideal science, and there is no good reason to think that current science is fundamentally wrong-headed, it can be used as a touchstone for identifying what counts as natural – even if this inventorying is only correlative.

This suggestion allows for what is a broad and anodyne way of describing Nature: it is all that would be susceptible of scientific investigation in ideal science. Does this mean that something has to be susceptible of scientific investigation in order to be natural? What if there was something that only obtains or subsists in relation to parts of Nature but that has no quantitative properties of its own by which to be studied by ideal science? Whatever such things would be – such as immaterial objects or properties – so long as they only existed *within* Nature, then nothing in what has been said would require introducing a new category of being just for them. In this way, what could be studied by ideal science is more of a guide to naturality than a litmus test. Appealing to this guide then, what sorts of things *could be* scientifically investigated in ideal science? Using current science as our touchstone for answering this question, at least two general categories of things should be recognized.

Whatever else Nature turns out to involve, it at least includes sensible reality: things which are of such a kind as to be in principle detectable by the senses (whether directly or indirectly

– as through sense-enhancing technologies – whereby we might see the microscopic or hear the ultra-sonic and so forth – or as predicted to exist by scientific theories, known to us in which case by an inferential chain of sensory links). All theorizing aside, we have found ourselves in a world that confronts us at every opportunity as sensible: though the sheer scale of the universe makes Nature as unfathomably full as it is empty, its innumerable objects and forms of being are susceptible of scientific investigation and so to some relevant extent, sensible.

But were Nature to include *only* sensible reality, it would not be *intelligible*: it could be sensed, but not understood. By taking science as our touchstone to understanding what is natural, we find the sensible, but in a second-order reflection we realize that the fact of science at all, let alone our use of it, takes for granted that the sensible is also intelligible. Without this supposition, we could see a tree, for example, but we would not understand that what we are seeing is a tree. Nor could we understand that what we are seeing is just *something or other*, though we may not know *what* exactly: there would be no understanding at all; our experiences would be void of any content; a sort of mindless beholding, or sheer presentness with no awareness beyond that fleeting immediacy. While we might be capable of such experiences, it goes without saying that most of our experiences are not like this: they are intelligible. As to what intelligibility involves, we should be comfortable taking for granted that Nature is un-controversially and pre-philosophically capable of being understood. Without this supposition, or something very much like it, no science (current, future or ideal) could exist or function beyond a robotic sort of going through of the motions, emptied of the first-person experience we have of doing so. In fact, the notion of intelligibility at play here will be so ground level that it would be presupposed in the very act of denying it. On this preliminary understanding of Nature then, it is both sensible and intelligible.

Consequently, for there to be more to reality than Nature there ought to be something which is minimally neither sensible nor intelligible because if it were either, while it might transcend parts of Nature, it would not transcend Nature *tout court*. Thus, for example, mental or moral properties might be thought to transcend various parts of Nature – such as space or time – but would nevertheless remain parts of Nature themselves because they only obtain or subsist in relation to yet other parts of Nature, such as embodied minds or actions. Likewise, if one were to transcend one hallmark of Nature after another but nevertheless remain *intelligible*, she will not have so separated herself from the boundaries of Nature that its inhabitants could not relate to her in the way they relate to any old part of Nature: through apprehension, understanding or comprehension. She would not fundamentally differ from how natural things are constructed in that minds could find in her what they find in everything else: a type of thing for one to be understood in terms of. She would be as an extreme, if anything, on a continuum or scale upon which all things fall, so that the difference between supernatural things and natural things is one of degree and not in kind, making the distinction ultimately non-fundamental. After all, she would only obtain or subsist *within* the matrix of relations that are home to the parts of Nature. When we speak of transcending Nature throughout this work, we intend a total transcending of Nature whereby it is a clean cut for one between her and a natural thing. Having developed some understanding of what it is to be natural and so by extension what it is that Gods would transcend, we can now ask what it means for something to be *in addition* to the sensible and the intelligible.

Just as we are concerned with what transcends Nature *tout court* rather than what only transcends some or most of Nature, so too are we concerned with what transcends sensibility and intelligibility *tout court* rather than with what only transcends some or most of either. As such, we shall say that to be *in addition* to the sensible, one should not be merely *practically* imperceptible whereby she goes undetected by instruments of sensation *because* of those instruments. She should be *inherently* imperceptible, so that she could not be detected *in principle*, by any possible instrument of sensation whatsoever. This latter sort of imperceptibility will boil down to not having any of the sorts of features by which one could be seen, heard, felt, smelled, tasted and so forth. In fact, and ultimately, such a one would not even have those features by which it could be studied by physics (quantum or otherwise), because even the most remote properties of physics are indirectly sensible.

Likewise, to be *in addition* to the intelligible is not merely for one to be inconceivable *in practice*, which would be due to a failure on our part to conceive rather than to an inability on her part to be conceived, but for one to be inconceivable *in principle*, which will boil down to not having any of those sorts of features by which one could be grasped by a mind. Much like most things will go undetected by a metal detector because there is nothing metallic about them, though they are no less real for that, the incomprehensible will go undetected by the mind because it is concept-less. To help illustrate what it would be to be concept-less, consider that if one were a type of thing, any type at all, she could then be conceptualized *as* that type of thing. Transcending intelligibility should be thought of as defying all *categorization*. But, to belong to no categories or to be no type of thing at all is for one to be *ineffable*; for there would be nothing about her beyond herself to describe her as. It should not go unnoted that on the view discussed so far, metaphysical Naturalism does not posit one less *kind* of thing than Theism does: the ineffable is not a type or category of thing at all.

It is here that we come into contact for the first time with the philosophical seed from which unfolds an entire polytheistic worldview: the ineffable. We began in this chapter by taking theism to hold that there is something which transcends *Nature* and have come to understand this claim to mean that in addition to the sensible and intelligible, there is the ineffable. But what is the ineffable?

Section 1.2: What is the Ineffable?

1. To be divine is to be beyond Nature.
2. **To be beyond Nature is to be henadic.**
3. To be henadic is to be polycentric.
4. Therefore, to be divine is to be polycentric.

At first pass, this question may appear rather innocent: if anything is ineffable, then what is it in virtue of which it counts as "ineffable?" Surely there is something that gives one the identity of being "ineffable" rather than, say, of being a human or a plant? Perhaps it is a transcendent nature or maybe even simply the property to transcend all things. But, if ineffability is about defying categorization, then ineffability should not be thought of as *another* category or type of thing.

When we think of 'what' something is, we can sometimes take it for granted that a distinction is being drawn between the thing and 'what' it is being thought of *as*. For example, if we think about what people are, we are looking for information *about* them and so for something that is in some sense not the same as them. More pointedly, one can only be a type of thing if *she* is around in the first place: the property of being a type of thing is something that is attributed to a subject; which implies that the subject *qua* subject, or the individual considered independent of being any type of thing, is *there* and so established with *some* sense of reality on her own, lest no one be around to bear the property of being a type of thing. As such, the very idea that one is a type of thing presupposes that there is more to her than just herself: there is, in addition, the type of thing that *she* is.

'Whats' are not just stark additions to who one is: they are what confers upon one the status of *being* the type of thing that she is. In other words, if one is intelligible *as* this or that sort of thing, it is because she *really* is this or that sort of thing. 'Whats' thus *make* things to be intelligible by *being* what is intelligible about them.

Some 'whats' add intelligibility to things by functioning as the blueprint for the organization of their parts. Here we could consider the multifarious parts of a human body, at whatever level of depth, and recognize that they continue to be organized according to a general pattern. But we can also see, through basic pattern recognition, that many numerically distinct individuals also have bodies which are being organized according to the same general pattern so that they all have something in common; something that is being repeated in or iterated among them which makes them intelligible as human beings. But, whether *all* 'whats' can be iterated among more than one individual or not, it is the fact that 'whats' are the sort of thing that are additions to who one is that will be our defining understanding of the 'what' unit as such.

The 'what' unit is paradigmatically represented by such things as properties, features, characteristics, propositions, states of affairs and in general any form of being at all. We may even find a sense of existence in which it is itself a 'what'; indeed, the most general of all 'whats', because every single thing that exists no matter how different has it in common at the very least that it is *some* type of thing or other. The most general type of thing that one can be is the type of thing that belongs to *a* type. On this notion of existence, we could treat ontology as that field concerned with the 'what' *qua* 'what' and its divisions into various sub-categories 'whats'.

As has been made implicit in the preceding, the 'what' unit can only be part of the equation: if it was all there were to reality, then there would be something that could be iterated but nothing around to iterate it; an absurd state of affairs that would rob 'iterability' and the like of its meaning. The idea here is that to be iterable, repeatable, replicable or the like just is for a 'what' to be instantiated or manifested in some possible world. But, if the actual world were populated *only* by the iterable, if it were iterables *all the way down*, then not only would there be no *actual* objects or relations around to instantiate any of the iterables, but there would be nothing in the actual world to constitute or provide an exemplification nexus for the emergence of such objects that would not itself just be another iterable: there would be nothing but iterables across the board. However, without even the *potential* for there to be anything to instantiate the iterables, the actual world would have no access relation to a possible world in which a 'what' is instantiated, rendering such a state of affairs impossible. As such, if it were iterables all the way down, there could be nothing to iterate them and they would not be iterable after all.

What-ness depends upon something else, which simply by virtue of not being a 'what', is peculiar, unique, individual, incommunicable to others and irreplicable. It is 'who' one is that things can be added to. The 'who' unit is paradigmatically represented by such things as the self or the subject *qua* subject. Whereas what-ness is intrinsically suggestive or implicative of who-ness, as the foregoing shows, who-ness is not intrinsically suggestive or implicative of what-ness. Peculiarity is first and foremost reflexive. Who-ness is thus irreducible to what-ness.

With these distinctions in mind we can return to the initial question: what is the ineffable? If we approach this matter as if there is some 'what' of which the ineffable is a 'who', we assert in one breath what we deny in the next: we say that something is ineffable and that it is not ineffable. For there to be a 'what' of which one is a 'who' just is for her to be effable *as* an instance of that type of thing. One might wish to suggest that this sort of effability is not at odds with ineffability, drawing a distinction between a deep and thin effability or some such. The idea here,

I would imagine, is that deep effability reflects a thing as it is in itself whereas thin effability reflects a thing as it is conceived or as it is conceivable or some such. But, introducing such a distinction will not challenge what has been said so far, so long as it is maintained that the ineffable as it is in itself cannot be an instance of any type of thing: it would be to treat the 'who' unit itself as an addition to the 'who' unit.

For all the foregoing reasons, ineffability is not to be thought of as a 'what'. But perhaps this will be seen as trivial or uninteresting since ineffability is in fact an apophatic term, saying of something what it is not rather than what it is. Is it not more interesting to consider that just as there is little more to silence than the absence of sound, or darkness the absence of light, perhaps there is little more to ineffability than the absence of intelligibility? On this understanding of ineffability, precious little could be deduced about one through her ineffability since all the information it conveys would be captured in the strictness of denial. But perhaps there is more to ineffability after all, and it is in fact one side to a coin, the other half of which is remarkably positive.

For one to not be any type of thing is for there to be nothing more to her than herself: were she to have anything added to her that is not just herself, such as properties, features or characteristics, she would be some type of thing; namely, the type of thing that bears those properties, features or characteristics. We shall refer to such a one throughout this work as a 'henad' or as being 'henadic', so that these terms will refer to one precisely in the respect in which she is a one for whom there is nothing more to her than herself. She is, as it were, purely 'who' she is and for that very reason, utterly ineffable. The foregoing will hopefully have put some meat on to our earlier assertion that to be ineffable is to defy all categorization: it is to be purely 'who' one is, without any 'whats' whatsoever.

But perhaps we can put more meat on the idea yet. Consider

that propositions are comprised of a subject and a predicate. Linguistically, subjects are *described* by predicates. As such, if we were to look at a subject without any predicates whatsoever, it would be *indescribable*. It is a categorical mistake to try and *describe* a subject without using predicates: we cannot *describe* subjects with subjects. The statement "Jack is Jill" does not *predicate* Jill or Jack. If anything, it *identifies* the two.

'Whos' are made intelligible or effable by their 'whats' just as subjects are made describable by their predicates. Conversely, as subjects are indescribable apart from predicates, so too are individuals *qua* individuals ineffable. This is not to suggest that in the absence of predicates subjects are just meaningless, empty symbols or that individuals are intrinsically devoid of identity: it is just that to *say* the subject is not to say anything descriptive *about* the subject. Not only is it a fallacy to infer without argument that because something lacks describable or effable content, it also therefore lacks any content whatsoever; it is an absurd view and one that is contrary to our experience. It is absurd because if no subject or individual is indescribable or ineffable, such as would be the case if subjects and individuals were *inseparable* or *indistinguishable* from predicates, then we cannot, either in fact or in principle, separate subjects or individuals from predicates in order to distinguish between the predicate and the subject of predication. This view thus collapses everything into predicates, leaving no room for anything to be the subject of predication. But, as we have seen in the case of there being nothing more to reality than 'whats', it cannot be predication *all the way down* because part of what it is to predicate *just is* to predicate *of something*. To preserve this most basic of distinctions then, we should grant that subjects and individuals are at least considered in and of themselves indescribable or ineffable. We shall use the subject-property structure of propositions as a tool throughout this work to better understand the ineffable.

One might wonder whether individuals are separable from

predicates in reality or whether the two can only be separated in our minds. But, if the two are inseparable *anywhere*, then somewhere there is predication *all the way down*, and we lose our most basic of distinctions. At least if this occurred in the mind there would still be individuals around to have minds predicated of them in reality but to have this collapse obtain in reality would be for things to be absurd in a way that we can scarcely comprehend. At the very least, we do not experience *ourselves* to be bundles of predicates, but as those who have things predicated of them.

Conclusion and Summary

We began this chapter with the commonsense impression of theism as the view on which there is more to reality than Nature: there is something that is not part of Nature, but in some way outside its boundaries. Section 1:1 began to unravel this impression and found that to be beyond Nature is to be ineffable. The idea here was just that whatever is outside of Nature altogether should be beyond the boundaries of whatever Nature includes. But Nature includes at least the sensible and intelligible. As such, whatever is beyond Nature will not be sensible or intelligible. But this is just for one to be ineffable. As such, we took theism to be the view that reality is not just sensible and intelligible, it is also ineffable. In Section 1:2, we found that to be ineffable is to be individual: it is to be as a subject *qua* subject, without any predicates to be described by. Putting our findings together, the internal logic of theism unfolded into the view that there is an individual beyond Nature; a henad, or one for whom there is nothing more to her than her*self*. This result places a curious qualification on philosophy: the discipline of thinking about or reflecting upon a particular henad will never deliver the information of who *she* is. This is because the information upon which we can chew and reflect through philosophy is not henadic: it would be like trying to figure out who a particular human being is by reflecting upon the properties of humanity. As Proclus says:

> Are we not making many declarations about the Demiurge and the other gods and even about the One itself? As an answer we might say that we speak about them, but we do not describe what they each are in themselves. We are able to speak scientifically, but not intuitively, (*On Timaeus*, II.303.18-22; 158)

In other words, the term 'henad' is being used as a collective singular, so that what is said of one henad is said of many henads. Finally, consider that the negation of theism (what we shall call atheism) will amount to a view on which there are no individuals beyond Nature. This way of framing the discussion is markedly different from standard protocol: the disagreement between the theist and atheist is not one over *what* types of things there are, but over *who* there is.

Chapter 2

Polytheism

1. To be divine is to transcend Nature.
2. To transcend Nature is to be henadic.
3. To be henadic is to be polycentric.
4. Therefore, to be divine is to be polycentric.

This chapter will continue to try and understand what theism amounts to and lead us to conclude that the third and final premise of this work's overarching argument is true: to be henadic is to be polycentric. The reader will recall that to be henadic is for one to be so utterly individual that all there is to her is herself. Such a one could not strictly speaking *have* properties, features, characteristics or anything of the sort because they are not ultimately *her*. The terms "henad" and "God" are used interchangeably, although "divine" is used stipulatively in premise (1) of the above argument and "henadic" is used speculatively in premise (2) of the same. I will defer elaboration of polycentricity to the rest of this chapter except to note by way of introduction and relevance that it is deeply, deeply polytheistic. Before diving into premise (3), we shall do as we have previously and state the idea behind the discussion to follow in as simple and condensed a form as we can:

The Gist: The henad does not belong to any kind or type no matter how general, let alone as its *only* member. As such, it can never be that any henad is the *only* henad: there is nothing for her to be the only one *of*. It follows that whichever henad theism affirms there to be, it cannot be the only one there is. Theism, in other words, just is polytheism. However, for there to be many henads is for them to have something in common, and as henads there is nothing for them to have in common but each other. Moreover, if they have each other in common, they cannot be extraneous to one another, lest there be more to a henad than herself. As such, the henads *have* each other in common by *being* each other. To be a henad is to be a way of being a multitude of henads; it is to be polycentric.

Section 2.1: Henadicity

For what those who understand [a] god's power do is not to reduce divinity to a single god but to show that divinity is as profuse as [a] god himself shows it to be ....

– Plotinus, Enneads II.9.35-38

Thus far, we have identified a basic way of stating theism – something transcends Nature – and found it to mean that there is an imperceptible, utterly unique individual: a henad, or God. This is a one for whom there is no answer to the question of what she is. While we are able to say that so-and-so is a human or that such-and-such is a golden retriever and so on and so forth, we are unable to say with truth that a God is *any* sort of thing. All there is to her is herself: she embodies no nature, bears no properties and instantiates nothing. She is beyond being and all its categories; she is purely who she is.

But is this notion of theism internally consistent? Are we not saying that one who is to be classified as a God is not to be classified as anything? And if someone can be both unclassifiable in principle and still a God, then what does it mean to say of one that she is "a God?" Though the answer is elegant in its simplicity, chewing on this sort of question will constitute the bulk of this chapter. Let us begin then with what has been established so far – the sheer, utter and pure individuality of the divine – and allow it to unfold according to its own internal logic.

Putting to use the conceptual tools developed earlier, we may ask of the predicate "a God" whether it signifies a 'who' or a 'what'. The reader will recall that 'what' represents anything that can be instantiated, exemplified, embodied or the like; it is typified by properties, features and characteristics and generally provides the answer to questions of 'what' something is. 'Who' is just the opposite and represents anything that is incommunicable, peculiar, unique, individual and is typified by the self or the subject *qua* subject. Now, if the divine predicate "a God" is a 'what', then according to what has just been said, it signifies something which is capable of being instantiated, exemplified or embodied: whether concrete or abstract, it will be the principle in a thing whereby it has the intelligibility of being a God. But, if one's identity as a God depends upon any such principle, then she will not transcend Nature: it will be one thing to consider her as subject *qua* subject and another to consider her as subject *qua* divine. Her divinity will be a complexifying predicate, as it were, or an extraneous appendage that will not figure into a consideration of 'who' she is or of her as subject *qua* subject.

The foregoing has brought to light a distinction between two sorts of predicates: both share a structural appearance, but one complexifies a subject while the other does not. That is, one attributes to a subject more than what is included in her as subject *qua* subject while the other does not. In non-complexifying predication, the predicate functions to specify the perspective from which the subject is being considered, e.g. subject *as* she is in herself, or *as* she is in another. Complexifying predication involves a division of *identities* between the subject and predicate, a sort of separation of or differentiation between the two. Non-complexifying predication involves a co-presence of *perspectives* between the subject and predicate such that an identity between the two is preserved. Complexifying predication destroys any hopes one would otherwise have of being ineffable and so divine. As such, however, else divinity is to be characterized, it cannot be as a 'what'. But in that case, how is it to be understood?

To clarify the problem at hand, if the predicate "a God" signifies a 'what', then it will represent something that is not the subject herself – such as a property, characteristic or feature – and will for *that* reason be excluded from a consideration of her as subject *qua* subject. But, the predicate "a God" does not signify a 'what'. As such, it is not excluded from a consideration of a God as subject *qua* subject. That is to say, to call one divine is to consider her precisely in the respect in which she is beyond Nature: it is, as it were, to say that she is purely 'who' she is.

What sense does it make then to say of any God that she is the only one? The only one of what? She has no kind. There is no such thing as a divine-making property, characteristic or feature in the first place, let alone for any number of individuals to have, still less by only one. To illustrate this from a slightly more analytic perspective, consider what can be called the monotheist proposition. This proposition encapsulates the idea of monotheism, and however else one expresses it, one should include an existential quantifier and an object of quantification. Without an existential quantifier, the sentence will not declare that there is any amount of anything, let alone that there is only one of something, thereby failing to capture or express the 'mono' aspect of monotheism. Without an object of quantification, the sentence will not specify that it is a God that is being declared to exist, thereby failing to capture or express the 'theism' aspect of monotheism. These grammatical conditions allow us to express the monotheistic proposition in different ways. Consider the following sentences:

1. There is only one God.
2. There is a God x and if anything is a God, then it is x.

Both (1) and (2) satisfy the relevant conditions and thus syntactically express the monotheist proposition. But there is more to propositional expression than just getting the grammar correct and so the monotheist proposition carries with it a semantic condition as well: whatever else the proposition means; it ought to be taken to oppose polytheism and atheism.

But as the reader will shortly come to see, combining these grammatical and semantic conditions results in a deeply confused position. To begin, consider each use of "God" in (1) and (2) and ask whether it is as a 'who' or as a 'what'. Perhaps it will come as a surprise to most readers that no possible combination results in a statement that opposes both polytheism and atheism. In other words, no statement can coherently or consistently express the grammar *and* the meaning of the monotheist proposition: it is not expressible without confusion or contradiction. To illustrate this, consider the following possible, representative combinations of 'who' and 'what' in (1) and (2):

1*. There is only one [of this God].
2*. There is [this God] x and if anything is [divine], then it is x.

Granted, there could not be more than one of a particular God. But this does not tell us whether or not there are *other* Gods, and so (1*) provides one with opposition to atheism but at the cost of being trivially compatible with polytheism. On the other hand, a divine-making property, characteristic or feature requires that there is more to a God than just herself, which means that she is effable and so not a God after all. In other words, (2*) provides nominal opposition to polytheism; but at the cost of even being theistic. As a result, monotheism is either trivially compatible with polytheism or materially equivalent with atheism.

Section 2.2: Polycentricity

...for all the henads are in each other and are united with each other, and their unity is far greater than the community and sameness among beings. In these too there is compounding of Forms, and likeness and

friendship and participation in one another; but the unity of those former entities, inasmuch as it is a unity of henads, is far more unitary and ineffable and unsurpassable; for they are all in all of them ...
– Proclus, *Parmenides* 1048, 10-15

Reason forbids us from asserting that there is only one God, but does it permit us to say merely that there is *a* God without committing to there being more than one? If there is a God, h1, and there cannot be only one God, then h1 cannot be the only God: there must be more. Theism, in other words, *just is* polytheism. True as this may be, the reason provided so far on its behalf is surface level compared to the polycentricity that will be the focus of the remainder of this section and to which we will now turn.

We have said that it can never be that any henad is the *only* henad: there is nothing for her to be the only one *of*. But, on the other hand, how could there be anything for the henads to be *many* of? The henad does not belong to any kind or type no matter how general, let alone as one among many. Whatever else the divine plurality involves, then, it cannot be a group united together by having some 'what' in common. Such plurality has one, exclusive center of unity, a 'what' that is instantiated, exemplified or embodied by each of the members. As Proclus says:

> Since, then, in every order there is some common element, a continuity and identity in virtue of which some things are said to be co-ordinate and others not, it is apparent that the identical element is derived by the whole order from a single originative principle. (Prop. 21)

This sort of plurality will be called monocentric plurality. Monocentric plurality is the plurality of Nature; it is the plurality that effable subjects enjoy. As such, it is a categorical

23

mistake to represent the divine manifold as a monocentric plurality, as would be the case if there was one, supreme God upon whom a group of lesser deities depended: such a view would hold what is beyond Nature to a standard of Nature. With that in mind, we may reason that either there is another sort of plurality appropriate to the divine, or there is not and the polytheism to which theism is committed can only be cashed out in contradictory or incoherent terms.

To begin sketching the conditions of a plurality appropriate to the ineffable, consider that in order to form any plurality whatsoever *something* must be held in common between one or more: it is just for there to be more than one *of something*; it is for some predicate F to apply to several or more subjects. Call this the commonality condition. Second, what a divine plurality has in common could not be a 'what': this would destroy their ineffability such that they would not turn out to be Gods after all. Call this the divine predicate condition. If one characterizes polytheism in a way that violates these conditions, she will have misrepresented polytheism. In the context of objecting to polytheism, this misrepresentation will constitute a straw-man fallacy. With these conditions in mind, we can turn now to wondering whether anything can satisfy them.

Since all there is to a henad is herself, there would be nothing for two or more of them to have in common but themselves. In doing so, the multiplicity would satisfy the commonality condition as well as the divine predicate condition: they would have something in common, and what they would have in common would not be a 'what'. But, what does it mean for the henads to have each other in common? Lest there be more to a henad than herself, the henads that she has in common with others cannot be *other* than herself. That is, they must be non-complexifying predicates which denote the subject herself and function to specify the perspective from which she is being viewed. If the henads, *as they are predicated of another henad*, are not that subject herself, there will be more to that subject than herself; namely, all these other henads. As such, the henads *have* each other in common by *being* each other: they are each a way of being all the others. This sort of plurality does not have one, exclusive center of unity: each henad is both that which is predicated of the others and that of which the others are predicated. Every God is both the center of which the others are a periphery and the periphery of which another is the center, the former being the God *qua* subject, the latter being the God *qua* non-complexifying predicate. They are all-in-each and each-in-all. The simultaneity of these perspectives in each henad render this sort of plurality *polycentric plurality*.

It may help to give a concrete example. Consider that according to polycentricity it is each God *qua* herself that is what all the other Gods have in common, rather than some 'thing', like a divine nature. That is, it is not *divinity* which the Gods have in common, but, say, Zeuseity, Odinity, Ganasheity, etc., depending on which God is in the subject position. And this is what it is for a God *qua* subject to function as a non-complexifying predicate: it is for, say, Zeus to function *as* Zeuseity. It could be said that *no* single God is privileged in this position, but it may be better to say that *each* God is privileged in this position. In Zeus, Odin is zeusical; in Odin, Zeus is odinical, as are all things, or so we shall argue in the next section. For now, we shall be content to conclude that part of what it is to be a henad at all *just is* to be an utterly unique way of being a multitude of henads, such that polytheism is included in the very notion of being a henad, ineffable or beyond Nature. As we shall see in the next chapter, polycentricity involves still more. In the words of Plotinus:

> For every god has everything in himself, and, again, he sees everything in another, so that everything is everywhere and all is all and each is all and the glory is unlimited. For each of them is great since even the small is great. (Enneads V.8.7-10)

Indeed, we shall find that each God individuates all things, making everything to be itself. So to the question one will perhaps be left asking of this section – just how many Gods are there? – we can only offer but a partial response here, for the answer comes in no small way from the fact of the Gods individuating all things. Let it suffice then to say this much, leaving the reader with the argument's reasoning and deferring support of its crucial premise to the next chapter: if the Gods individuate all things, then they individuate number as well. If they individuate number, then number does not precede deity. And if number does not precede deity, then it is not what affixes itself to the number of Gods there are, determining them to be of this or that amount: they would be intrinsically indeterminate.

Conclusion and Summary

We began this chapter by reflecting on the radical individuality of the henad and raised a concern about the internal consistency of theism: how can one be both unclassifiable *as* anything and still be *a* God? As we discovered in Section 2.1, to call one "a God" is not to attribute to her any divine-making property, characteristic or feature: it is to say of one that she is purely 'who' she is. This led us to consider the monotheist proposition and we found it inexpressible, collapsing under analysis as it did into either polytheism or atheism. With the impossibility of monotheism in place, we deduced that theism just is polytheism. But, does polytheism fare any better? The viability of theism depends on it. In Section 2.2 we maintained a consistency of method and applied the same pressure to polytheism that we applied to monotheism, determining that the integrity of its content depended on whether plurality could ever be polycentric. Our investigation found that henadicity naturally and seamlessly satisfies the conditions of polycentricity. Having led these notions to their logical conclusions, whatever those turned out to be, we have found that the third premise of this work's overarching argument is true: to be henadic is to be polycentric.

Chapter 3

The Procession of Being

1. To be divine is to transcend Nature.
2. To transcend Nature is to be henadic.
3. To be henadic is to be polycentric.
4. Therefore, to be divine is to be polycentric.

We have come to a working, ground-level understanding of what theism amounts to and have it in place now that theism just is polytheism. But, in deviating from standard protocol for works of this sort, we have yet to say much about what the Gods are like. While there is indeed much to be said about the matter, we shall try to stay in keeping with the general project of this work by avoiding verbose and dense expositions, especially if they veer from our simple intent of looking at things in the big picture from the theist perspective. With this intent in mind, we shall enrich our understanding of the Gods by investigating how all things relate to them. Our method will remain that of allowing the unifying logic of theism to unfold for itself and answer our questions along the way. Having explained and established each premise in the work's overarching argument, we can now draw the conclusion: to be divine is to be polycentric. While this conclusion includes everything that has been said about polytheism thus far, we have in many ways only begun to scratch the surface and it will be our task throughout this chapter to tap into some of the depth and richness of this proposition.

For those who are coming into this chapter without having looked into the previous sections, to be henadic is to be so utterly individual that all there is to one is herself, and to be polycentric is for it to be a part of 'who' each henad is that she is a unique way of being a multitude of henads. We shall continue to employ the subject-predicate model to understand how the Gods are in each other. Of the conceptual tools introduced so far, three will play a large role in the investigations to follow: the 'what', the 'who' and the non-complexifying predicate. The 'what' encompasses anything that can be instantiated, exemplified, embodied or the like; it is paradigmatically represented by properties, features and characteristics and generally provides the answer to questions of 'what' something is. 'Who' is just the opposite and encompasses anything that is incommunicable, irreplicable, unique, individual or the like; it is paradigmatically represented by the self or the grammatical subject *qua* subject and generally provides the answer to questions of 'who' someone truly is. Finally, the non-complexifying predicate is a predicate which signifies the subject rather than something about her and specifies the perspective from which she is being considered.

Polycentricity reaches depths we have not yet approximated, and it will be the task of this chapter to let that notion run its natural course on through to its logical conclusions and bring to light how all things relate to the Gods. As we have with the premises beforehand, we shall state the idea behind our conclusion as it relates to our discussion in as simple and condensed a form as we can before unpacking it:

The Gist: Each God is both the subject of whom the other Gods are predicated and a predicate for whom another God is the subject. *Qua* subject, the God is incommunicable and functions as a 'who'. But, *qua* predicate, she is communicable and functions as a 'what'. The introduction here of 'what' represents the most general layer of Nature. Each level of generality in Nature is constituted by a corresponding level of generality in the subject-predicate structure among the Gods. Just as each God is at once both subject and predicate, so too is she at once both predicable as such and predicated of another; at once predicated of this specific group of Gods and predicated of that God in particular.

The unifying logic that stratifies each deity is the polycentric structure which inherently involves this organization, and this layering goes on until the bottom of the manifold has been reached, so to speak, and no further predication can take place. In this way, the Gods are not just unique ways of being each other but of being all things.

Section 3.1: Divine Constitution

Why, then, should one not describe this activity of the One as motion? Because, I would say, one should not rank activity as prior to essence, nor in general grant activity to the first principle, ... And we shall not wonder how all things arise from the One without its acting. For it is possible to argue that that which produces something by acting experiences this through deficiency of power; of a superior nature is that which produces in virtue of its existence alone; this thing, then, will be free of the burdens of creation.
– Proclus, *Parmenides* 1167, 16-18; 1168, 1-5.

We have devoted relative length to considering the Gods as subjects: they are idiosyncratic, peculiar and entirely themselves. But we have not yet paid much attention to the Gods as predicates. Our reflections on the former brought to light a number of important theses relating to theism, especially when it came to the idea of the Gods being in each other as well as the logistics involved in that, it is our hope that such a reflection on the latter will unveil similarly crucial truths about how all things are full of Gods.

Let us begin by recalling that the subject *qua* subject does not take the predicate into account: this is why she is indescribable or ineffable; she has nothing to be described *by*. In a similar way, the predicate *qua* predicate involves no subject, or no subject *in particular* at least. After all, we are talking about *the* predicate as such rather than a particular example of one, and so by extension *the* subject as such rather than a particular example of one. In this position the predicate signifies something that is communicable to and predicable of another, and these properties make it so that it functions as a 'what': it denotes something that can be *in* another. We say that the predicate as such *functions* as a 'what' rather than that it *is* a 'what' because not all predicates can be said to denote 'whats' without qualification. The non-complexifying predicate, for example, *is* a predicate, but it nevertheless signifies the subject, just not *as* she is in herself. In other words, because it signifies a 'who', such a predicate is not simply a 'what'. But because it functions as a 'what', it is not simply a 'who' either. The transition from 'who' to 'what' here, or of a God from being a subject to a predicate, represents a decline from the sheer ineffability of the subject *qua* subject. It is a transition between modes of individuality and takes place *within* a God such that it is *she* who takes on the role of 'what'. Each God constitutes a 'what' in taking on this role because there is nothing more for her to do so with than her utterly simple self: she *is* whatever she *does*. As such, she constitutes things in her own henadic way; that is, *as* a 'who'. The 'what' is not some property, characteristic or feature of hers but rather 'who' she is in the predicable position.

To see a contradiction in the non-complexifying predicate as both signifying a 'who' *and* constituting a 'what' is to do an injustice to how perspectival polycentricity is. The 'what' has a self *as the 'what' that it is*, an integrity of *being* itself. The reality of this vantage point or ontological first-person perspective – if we can abstract the notion of 'self' within the first-person perspective from any association of it with consciousness or the like – is the deepest aspect of oneself, and it is true from that view that it is itself, in this case a 'what'. But what makes it *to be* itself, what establishes and secures its identity as itself, is that it is *included* in each Gods' self; it is included in 'who' each of them is. This is how the God can be 'who' the 'what' is without reducing or dissolving its perspective into hers.

Because the predicable position as such relates one to *any* given subject whatsoever rather than to any one in particular, each God *qua* predicate constitutes at this level the deepest most abstract 'whats' possible, such that they could be instantiated, exemplified or embodied by *any* natural subject whatsoever. It is not our concern here to identify which 'whats' these are and what has been said will apply no matter what they turn out to be, if there even are more than one most general 'what'. Whatever the case may be, the 'whats' at this level of reality are so general and abstract that anything would have them in common simply by virtue of their being anything at all. At this level of stratification, the Gods *qua* predicable are providing the very defining structures of existence *qua* 'what' itself.

It should not go unnoticed that the natural subject as such just effortlessly fell out of our discussion: its introduction is anything but *ad hoc* and testifies to the generativity of the subject-predicate structure among the Gods: it is the engine behind the procession of reality. Because the God *qua* predicate is predicated of the God *qua* subject, the natural subject that she inherently implies is constituted by the God *qua* subject.

How is it that the God *qua* predicate *and* the God *qua* subject constitute reality? While it is true that each God *qua* predicate constitutes reality, she only does so as she is *in* another God. As such, without detracting in the least from the reality of her constitution in the predicate position, it is in the subject position that each God ultimately constitutes all of reality, because it is there in that position where all of divine constitution *takes place*.

A further decline from henadic ineffability occurs as the God *qua* predicable transitions to the God *qua* predicated. Here the perspective shifts from the predicate as it is in *itself* to the predicate as it is in *another*. At this depth, the most general kinds and types – even that of existence itself *qua* 'what' – are *instantiated*: the predicables are predicated and Nature takes shape. No matter the details, Nature clearly teems with the sensible and the intelligible. We are simply looking at them only insofar as they exist, or are natural, and so forth, abstracting such commonalities from their particular details and all but ignoring their specificities for the time being.

It is important to emphasize that this is a level of reality rather than an event at some point in time: it is that layer of any thing's makeup at which it is in the most general sense a mixture or combination of 'who' and 'what'. This emphasis will safeguard us from making two errors. First, we should not think of the grounding provided for by the Gods as a *creation*: the Gods are not *doing* anything, strictly speaking, they are simply *being*. As such, it takes no time for the Gods to constitute things, they are hardly performing an *action* in the conventional sense of the term here. In this vein, they undergo no change in constituting things as they otherwise would if they transitioned from a state of not doing so to doing so. Second, and on a related note, it is not as if the Gods grounded Nature in some initial state in order to get things going, so to speak, only to then withdraw and allow the machine to run on its own: there could be nothing around to do anything if the Gods were not there providing the ground for it to be itself at every moment in which it is. In the words of Proclus:

> All things are bound up in the gods and deeply rooted in them, and through this cause they are preserved in being; if anything falls away from the gods and becomes utterly isolated from them, it retreats into non-being and is obliterated, since it is wholly bereft of the principles which maintain its unity, (Prop. 144).

As the polycentric structures continue the pattern of descent into greater complexity, the Gods individuate each thing at more levels of their constitution until their every aspect derives its integrity as itself from the Gods: they make the necessary to be necessary, the contingent to be contingent and the physical to be physical; they make anything and everything no matter what it is to be itself.

One might wonder whether the list of things which the Gods could individuate is independently determined such that the Gods can only individuate whatever *happens* to be individuatable. But as Proclus says, "[e]very god is a measure of things existent" (Prop. 117). The polycentric manifold provides the very parameters within which to define what it even means *to be*, and so all the more what it means to be *this* or *that* sort of thing. They impart all unity or individuality to absolutely everything at every single moment by *being* absolutely everything at every single moment: it is 'who' they are. This is the way in which all things proceed from and are constituted by the Gods. It is a sort of blooming of all that was contained within the seed of ineffability, a blooming that stretches across time and space until it finds rest in the final unfolding of the contents of reality, a point that corresponds to the polycentric structure in which, for each God, one specific deity "h1" is predicated of another specific deity "h2." As Proclus says, "[a] god is more universal as he is nearer to the One, more specific in proportion to his remoteness from it," (Prop. 126).

The aspirations of this work do not exceed the simple intention of giving one an idea of how all things look in the big picture from the theist perspective, and so it is not our hope to *map* the procession of being in any sort of exhaustive way. There are indeed many moments in the grand emanation of all things. For example, the layer of reality just discussed was found to involve any God simply insofar as she is predicated. But, what about specific Gods insofar as they are predicated? One God will not be the same in the predicated position as another even though they are both predicated of all the others, and so here we would see a further specification in a thing's constitution wherein it is not just a combination of 'who' and 'what' in the most general sense, but of some one or more specific 'whats'. What about any God whosoever insofar as she is predicated of this or that specific group of Gods, or a specific deity predicated of the same? The possible combinations of pantheons are numerous and indicate how thorough and immediate divine constitution is. At each succeeding level, the relevant polycentric structure does the work of making its corresponding layer of reality to be whatever or whoever it is, down to the most minute detail.

We have it in place now that part of what theism amounts to is the position that the Gods constitute everything. As Proclus said, "each of the gods is the universe in his own different way," (*On Timaeus*, II.308.3-4; 162). To address possible or remaining concerns about what this *means*, we can offer the following considerations. We have chosen to risk making it sound more obscure and complicated than it really is in order to present this idea in today's language with its unique concerns. But what this really all boils down to is that the Gods function as the 'form' of Self for each thing, no matter what, simply insofar as it is itself. It is by participating in this 'form' that each thing has the integrity of being itself. By functioning as a sort of 'formal' cause for each thing at every level, the Gods *constitute* everything. For Zeus, all things are participants of Zeuseity, and unique ways of being zeusical. For Odin, all things are participants of Odinity, and unique ways of being odinic. Each God constitutes an exhaustive and complete cosmos wherein she is the ultimate form of Self for each self. As such, she cannot be identified with just any one thing. Her utterly peculiar and abiding 'self' *is* all things, not *this* 'what' or *that* combination of 'who' and 'what': *all* things. Neither is her 'self' some stand-alone 'who' established *apart from* all things which then attaches to them in some manner, everything is a participation of her 'self' so that she is a completely and utterly irreplicable way of *being* everything. Nor are the Gods collections of things. Any such notion requires that the Gods are combinations of 'who' and 'what' and separates them from all things in such a way that a God's *self* is here on the one hand and all things are there on the other, relating the two in some combinatorial way, like body is to mind or like matter is to form or some such.

Addressing this sort of concern will be especially important for those who are under the impression from the preceding that while theism just is polytheism, polytheism just is pantheism. To avoid needless controversy over terminology, we shall address this concern only inasmuch as it is of concern, namely, insofar as it refers to a position which naturalizes the Gods by relating them to Nature in such a way that it makes them effable. To find such a position in any of what has been said is to have severely misunderstood: the deep immanence of divine constitution *secures* the transcendence of the Gods. Consider, for example, that the way in which they *are* all things requires that they *precede* all things: the one stratified must precede the stratifications. Because it is part of her utterly unique self that she is all things, she cannot be limited to any one of them, either in part or in whole. If she were limited to any of them in part, she would not be all things in *any* sense; but, if she were limited as the whole of which all things are parts, then she would only be all things in the sense of a 'what', and not a 'who'. Having said that, divine constitution *is* deep and involves an intimacy, intensity and immediacy of connection between the divine and all things that many – both professing theist and atheist alike – will undoubtedly be unaccustomed to thinking in terms of.

Was it not recommended to think of the Gods as the form of Self for each self? Would this not lend itself to an articulation of pantheism on which the divine is the form and Nature the matter? No. Such a view makes all things into a whole of which one part is the divine and the other is Nature. This is antithetical to all that has been said so far. Inasmuch as Gods function as the form of Self for each self, there could not be any self already around for the Gods to impress the form of Self upon: theirs would not be just another case of making matter to be in a form, but of making matter and form to be in the first place: they constitute all things in a far more radical way and extend to everything from the ground up, as it were. Having derived and developed the idea of the procession of being from the Gods with the level of precision and depth that is proportionate to our purpose, it seems we are prepared to move on in the next section to glean what information we may about what the Gods are like by returning once more to the wellspring of insight that is polycentricity.

Section 3.2: Divine Predicates

Every attribute of the gods pre-subsists in them in a manner consonant with their distinctive character as gods, and since this character is unitary (prop. 113) and above Being (prop. 115), they have all their attributes in a unitary and supra-existential mode.

– Proclus, Prop. 118

So far, we have found that the Gods make each thing to be itself: they individuate 'whos' by constituting them in the subject position and 'whats' by constituting them in the predicate position. In this way, each thing – whether a 'who' or a 'what' – may be thought of as an embodiment of a henad, such that part of what it even means to be anything at all is to be the bearer of a henad's distinctive character or her unity. But, this way of putting things is not entirely satisfactory from a perspective of conceptual precision because it is more the case that a thing's self is what a henad looks like through the lens of limitation than that a thing's self is in some way independently established, albeit intrinsically containing or imitative of a henad. With that expressive difficulty in mind, we can proceed to use such looser language.

Having it now in place that the Gods individuate all things, we can briefly return to the question left partially unaddressed in the last chapter as to how many Gods there are. Recall that as we noted there, to individuate all things, the Gods will need to individuate even number itself. But, in so doing, the Gods will precede number so that their amount will be undetermined *by* a specific number. This is not to say that their amount is *undetermined*, only that it is not a *number* that determines it: the Gods could not be subordinated to anything that is not itself a God. In this way, we should not wonder whether there is some arbitrary number of Gods (such as 243) or whether considerations of simplicity have any bearing on how many Gods we ought to assent to there being – it may be that we should posit no more than is needed to explain the data, but we are not positing anything; we are just watching the rules of logic unfold more implications.

As we have seen in this chapter, the Gods individuate all things because they are that by participation in which a thing is itself. Accordingly, each God imparts to the numbers their very identities as the numbers that they are. It is therefore not the numbers which count the Gods, so to speak, but the Gods which count the numbers. That is, in a view on which deity precedes number rather than the other way around, the Gods are primarily that by which we count things so that the Gods themselves are not determined to be of this or that amount *by* something that is not itself a God – such as an abstract object. With these considerations in place, we can resume our discussion.

The more general or abstract a thing, the less limitations there will be to constrain its depiction of 'who' a henad is. But, everything, no matter its degree of limitation, is a window into 'who' a henad is. Herein we encounter an important consequence of divine constitution: the revelatory nature of all things. The concept of an inherently revelatory Nature simply falls out of a consideration of polytheism and should not go unnoted. Nature is more of an *encounter* with the Gods than it is a book containing doctrinal, propositional truths concerning theism and could very well explain the sacred, noumenal, enchanting impression of Nature so often associated with Paganism. The revelatory nature of all things provides a method for answering the question of what the Gods are like.

Yet it may strike the reader as odd, to ask of one for whom there is nothing more to her than herself, "What is she like?" The question appears to assume that the henads have properties, features or characteristics to ponder about. Inquiring after the divine in this manner is not at all unusual in the philosophy of religion: is the divine omnipresent, omniscient, omnipotent or good? Such talk of the so-called divine attributes is not out of place here, as we shall soon see, but it must be kept in mind that the divine predicates are the henads themselves rather than independently established 'whats' which the Gods then instantiate or exemplify. Because each God is in all the Gods, and each God constitutes a 'what', all 'whats' are included in each God, such that, for example, so long as there *are* such 'whats' as knowledge, power and goodness, then knowledge, power and goodness are *in* each God. And because there can be nothing more to each God than herself, then the way in which each God *has* knowledge, power and goodness is by *being* them.

Looking at 'whats' as images of the invisible, each henad can be seen as the ones of whom, say, knowledge, power and goodness are but finite representations of. This is to say that such attributes would belong to the Gods, but after *their* non-complexifying, henadic manner, and so undetermined by the sensible, intelligible boundaries of Nature. What has been said so far applies to any other 'what' as well and provides a general method for coming to understand what the Gods are like. For example, one could only find that the Gods are impersonal, mechanical principles of individuation at the cost of having to say that *nothing* is robustly personal; for inasmuch as there is such a thing as being 'personal', it will be individuated as such because a henad stands in the relevant, corresponding position.

But, because each henad is a way of being all the others, no henad could constitute the 'what' of the personal without all the henads doing so as well, each in their own way. Reality is a consensus of the Gods. As such, because everything is individuated as itself through divine constitution, all attributes will be finite, divided expressions of infinite, undivided henads.

But as a means of learning about what the Gods are like, the revelatory nature of all things is rather *a posteriori* and not in keeping with the general methodology of this work. Just as we were not satisfied to present, develop and defend polytheism in Chapter 2 on the basis of a foreign methodology – viz. through a sort of process of elimination by objecting to monotheism – but instead sought deeper, positive grounding by allowing the inner logic of theism to unfold for itself, so too will we be unsatisfied here to learn about what the Gods are like by using a bottom-up approach which reasons to the Gods and not from them.

Consider then the obvious way in which the Gods can be called omnipresent: they are *present* in some substantive way to the things they *constitute*. Of course, they are not present in a natural manner because they are not themselves natural: theirs is not a sensible or intelligible presence, which in one way or another has something to do with which complexifying predicates a subject *has* – e.g. one can have a sensible presence by occupying this or that space or an intelligible presence by being on another's mind and so forth – but rather an ineffable presence, which has instead to do with the non-complexifying predicate that a subject *is* – e.g. a subject may function as the 'what' of life, making her present in every living thing inasmuch as their identity as such is but a function of sharing in her unity so that their genuine and subsisting selves just are what she looks like through the lens of a specific combination of limitations.

In a similarly pithy fashion, it can be said that the Gods are omniscient, for in giving to each thing its very identity, the Gods comprehend within themselves the content of each thing's identity, whether that content is propositional or qualitative. Of course, because they are not themselves natural, theirs is not a natural sort of knowledge; discrete, tensed, dependent or involving change. As Proclus says:

> Every god has an undivided knowledge of things divided and a timeless knowledge of things temporal; he knows the contingent without contingency, the mutable immutably, and in general all things in a higher mode than belongs to their station, (Prop. 124).

Moreover, because nothing exists in any way unless it is divinely constituted, the Gods hold each thing in being at every moment that it exists. But surely, that upon which all things *depend* is in some remarkable sense *powerful*. The divine sphere of influence whereby all things are individuated is all-encompassing, and this is through the interconnectivity of polycentricity in which each God is the site where the divine constitution of all things takes place. And so, theirs is not an activated ability or an exertion of force; it is no feat of strength or endurance for them to hold all things in existence. These and other cases of natural power derive their character as such from the ones whom they are the limited depictions of; the subject-predicate structure among the Gods wherein each God is, non-complexifyingly, all-predicated or all-powerful.

Finally, and as we shall see in the next chapter, because procession is something that is directed toward bringing about some outcome or result and all things proceed from each God, all things are directed toward each God as toward the end for which they proceed. As such, it is the case that each God is not only what all things proceed *from*; and so, the originating principle of all things, but also what all things proceed *toward*, and so the final end of all things. In this way, all things are attracted or drawn to the Gods, driven toward them as to the whole point of their being here at all. In constituting their ultimate or final end, each God provides all things with their deepest sense of normativity and purpose. Moreover, the divine constitution instills each thing with its identity so that while things might go on to do bad for others or be harmful to or incompatible with each other, the Gods only give a thing what is most good for it: its self. Surely what all things strive to obtain and indeed the very point or end of their procession, which bestows upon each thing only what is most good for it, is itself good in a deeply rich and significant way (cf. Prop. 13).

For all that has been said about the Gods possessing the traditionally identified divine attributes, it should be kept in mind that divine constitution involves a stratification in each God whereby she can be *seen*, so to speak, through the lenses of Nature. So beheld, it may not occur to one to attribute to a deity such omni-attributes: it may be that one does not see who a deity is *in herself* through an experience of her *in Nature*. Whether that experience is undergone directly by one or learned of through another's testimony, such as when recorded in mythic or literal terms, we should not expect *all* who encounter the Gods in Nature to look beyond their particular constitutions. In this way, it should not be surprising then if there were various polytheist cultures or religions that did not or do not regard each of the Gods as all-knowing, all-powerful or all-good.

In closing this section, I will make the following remarks about the problem of evil. So much of today's discussions and debates in the philosophy of religion revolve around who, if anyone, is ultimately responsible or to blame for evil. But, according to the account of theism so far presented, reality does not unfold from the Gods by a decision: it is not up to the Gods to be 'who' they are, and part of 'who' they are *just is* the polycentric manifold with its attending subject-predicate structure that *just is* Nature. The Gods emanate reality by nature, so to speak, not by choice and this emanating process continues until a layer of reality is reached where one is as far from the pure individuality of the Gods as one can get before having no identity whatsoever of her own. On this precipice into nothingness, participation in the Gods is intermittent, so that part of its characterization as a stage of procession is the flickering participation of its inhabitants. Inasmuch as the divine constitution of all things provides them with normativity and purpose, the absence of the Gods in things through their intermittent participation is contrary to how things are supposed to be, and so evil becomes inevitable at this final stage of the procession. However, whichever level of Nature evil arises in, we should not demand that the Gods have a morally sufficient reason for permitting evil to exist at all: *decisions* are made by creatures, not by Gods.

Conclusion and Summary

We began this chapter by reflecting on the Gods *qua* predicates. It was found that because predicates inherently function as 'whats', the Gods themselves function as 'whats'. In so doing, the Gods *constitute* 'whats' and therefore the architecture of Nature. Had there been such a thing, and 'whats' were included in 'what' the Gods are instead of 'who' they are, their inclusion could have allowed for a reduction whereby 'whats' are *really* just the Gods in the final analysis; as when a body can be considered in ever more reductive terms – say, as a collection of cells, atoms, then sub-atomic particles and so forth and so forth. But, as it stands, 'whats' are included within the Gods after the latter's mode of unity, which is not just *another* type of being for the former to be understood in terms of: it is not a type of being at all. This distinction allowed us to distinguish divine constitution from a simplistic sort of pantheism.

Moreover, 'whats' *just are* the structures of which Nature, through all its profuse instantiations, is comprised: they provide Nature with its intelligibility and by extension its sensible exemplifications. But, just as the divine predicates take divine subjects, and the former constitute natural predicates, so too do natural predicates take natural subjects, and the latter constitute them. In this way, Nature derives in every way and at every moment from the Gods. As we noted at the start, each level of generality in Nature is constituted by a corresponding level of generality in the subject-predicate structure among the Gods so that the most general sort of 'whats' are constituted by the Gods precisely insofar as they are predicable all the way down to the most specific sort of 'whats' being constituted by one specific deity being predicated of another. Section 3.1 drew a distinction between divine constitution and divine creation by noting that as the polycentric structure just *involves* the Gods being in the predicate position relative to each other, so too and for this very reason does it just *involve* the existence of Nature.

In Section 3.2 we found that the flip-side of divine constitution meant that Nature is inherently revelatory of 'who' the Gods are so that by looking to what exists, it can be seen that it is but a finite and divided expression of one who is infinite and undivided. Fascinating and important as it is, by providing the reader with a method rather than results, we were able to preserve the pithy and accessible genre this work was intended to be part of. Indeed, in keeping with this simple intention, we went on to reason from the Gods rather than to them and came to understand a sense in which the Gods are all-knowing, all-powerful and all-good. We ended the section and chapter with a discussion about evil and how typical ways of framing the issue are not really all that relevant to the system of theism presented and discussed here: questions of responsibility are like fish out of water in a context of emanation.

Chapter 4

Religion

The preceding chapters followed a format in order to clarify what theism amounts to and how all things look according to its picture of reality. In doing so, we were able to organize our discussions by expounding the premises and conclusions of an overarching argument that delivered a view on which all things are divinely constituted by a plurality of polycentric henads. Having presented and developed this view, we no longer need to expound that argument or any other and so have no need to thematize our discussion by heading it with premises or conclusions. But there is still a question that remains to be answered and that is what theism and its picture of reality mean for mankind. In light of all that has been said, what we are looking for in more precise terms is what it means for us that all things are constituted by a plurality of polycentric henads. Of course, while there are other facets of the image on the puzzle box to which we could draw attention, particularly in relation to the subject of this final chapter, we shall focus upon that among them which seems most important to talk about if given the opportunity. In other words, while the reality of divine constitution by a plurality of polycentric henads means quite a lot of things for us, and our inquiry will proceed according to the same methodology and rubric of brevity and clarity that has governed our material from the start, this closing chapter will focus on the Gods as the Good and what relations this cultivates.

It is not recommended that one come to this portion of the work without having at least familiarized herself with the notions from the preceding chapters. Bearing these remarks in mind, we can now begin. Although we are no longer following the format of expounding a proposition in an overarching argument, we shall nevertheless continue our practice of summarizing the gist of the discussion to follow:

The Gist: Where all things are constituted by a plurality of polycentric henads, everything is in constant and utter dependence upon the Gods. As parts of Nature, people owe it to the Gods that they exist at all, let alone from one moment to the next. Our utter helplessness to even exist on our own is not only met with an abiding constancy, but with a superabundance of everything else we receive that is good beyond that. How people should relate to the Gods in light of this unmerited generosity comes down to what the Gods deserve. By reflecting on what justice is for others in general, we come to a better understanding of what justice is for the Gods in particular and we find that trying to do right by the Gods for all they are and do for us is the heart of religion. These conclusions are cemented in results gleaned from our now familiar *a priori* methodology, according to which it is found that because procession is something which is directed toward bringing about some outcome or result and all things proceed from each God, all things are directed toward each God as toward an end such that the Gods provide all things with their deepest sense of normativity and purpose.

Section 4.1: Justice for Any

Justice is a habit of mind which gives every man his desert while preserving the common advantage. Its first principles proceed from nature, then certain rules of conduct became customary by reason of their advantage; later still both the principles that proceeded from nature and those that had been approved by custom received the support of religion and the fear of the law. The law of nature is that which is not born of opinion, but implanted in us by a kind of innate instinct: it includes religion, duty, gratitude, revenge, reverence and truth. Religion is that which brings men to serve and worship a higher

order of nature which they call divine.
– Cicero, II. Liii

Cicero's remarks here reflect the common idea among ancient Graeco-Roman moralists that justice is a habit of mind; a sort of disposition to think certain things. As he indicates, the first principles of this habit do not arise by convention but inhere within us as "a kind of innate instinct", the first of which to be mentioned is called religion. The natural instinct to serve and worship "a higher order of nature" is a principle of justice because such is *owed* to what "they call divine." As it was passed down through the ages that religion is a form of the virtue of justice – viz. a good habit – the idea entered into a vast discussion between different thinkers about what a virtue is, what justice consists in and whether anything other than the divine could be the object of the virtue of religion. Over the course of centuries, the idea was increasingly refined by generation after generation of sustained critical thought, and this particularly so by the Scholastic philosophers who took the field in the Middle Ages. In a heyday of appropriating pagan thought for monotheist purposes, the Scholastics produced a vast literature on the subject of the virtue of religion as it had come to them from the ancient Graeco-Roman moralists and their treatments range from Suarez's monumental 1,100-page tome in the *Vivés Opera Omnia*, to a variety of Scholastic manuals on theology and ethics, such as Regatillo-Zalba's *Theologiæ Moralis*. Needless to say, by the time the ideas of the ancient schools had trickled down to the Scholastic thinkers, they were devastatingly incomplete and being ransacked for serviceable parts in an attempt to bolster monotheist thought. But for all that, and to its everlasting credit, even the grains of Platonic wisdom which made it to the Scholastics during this period fueled their wonder and brought philosophical life to whatever they touched.

Among these later thinkers, none is more foundational or

accessible than Thomas Aquinas who delivers his lengthiest treatment of the matter in the *Summa Theologiæ* (S.T.). Aquinas takes a classical idea of justice and explicitly considers, in typical clarity, how we ought to relate to the divine and we shall outline his presentation in order to guide our own reflections on the matter. Still, we shall have need in what follows to pry certain ideas from the monotheist context in which he situated them. However, the reader may be surprised at how rarely this is required, and by how easy it is done.

The classical view of justice which Aquinas expands on can largely be found in Nichomachean Ethics V by Aristotle, his philosophical exemplar, and may be summarized as follows: a virtue is a habit or disposition toward what is good (S.T. I.II.55.3-4). A virtue is said to be intellectual if it is a disposition of the intellect and moral if it is a disposition of the will (S.T. I.II.58.3). Insofar as the good to which a virtue directs us can be known to be good by reason, the virtue may be acquired through disciplined effort. The good to which the virtue of justice directs us can be known to be good by reason (S.T. II.II.58.1) and therefore can be acquired through disciplined effort.

But is justice an intellectual virtue or a moral virtue? In other words, is justice a habit of the intellect or of the will? According to Aquinas, "we are said to be just through doing something aright, and because the proximate principle of action is the appetitive power, justice must needs be in some appetitive power as its subject." That is, to be just is to do what is right. But since actions are caused by desires, justice must be caused by some sort of desire. So, in which of our appetitive powers must justice reside? Justice properly directs man in his relation to others (S.T. I.II.57.1). That is, justice concerns how we ought to relate to others – viz. doing what is right by others. As such, whichever appetitive power of ours is the one in which justice resides, whether it is the desires of the mind or the desires of the body, it must be able to desire such generalized things as a relation of one to another. But, the desires of the body do not hunger for such generalized things, because they take as their objects the limited and particular information we acquire through our sense apprehensions, and so the sense desire "does not go so far as to be able to consider the relation of one thing to another," (S.T. II.II.58.4). In other words, we can only sensually desire what we know through our senses and what we know through our senses are sensations such as a temperature, texture or taste. As such, we can only sensually desire sensations, and the relation of one thing to another is not a sensation. By disjunction, Aquinas deduces that justice must reside in the will or the desires of the mind, which can and does take such generalized things because it acquires its objects from the intellective power to apprehend general information.

Section 4.2: Justice for the Gods

Having developed a preliminary sense of what justice is, such that it is how we should relate to others, we can turn now to discussing whether there is a way we ought to relate to the Gods. According to Aquinas, God is among those whom the virtue of justice directs us to render what is due because "[*inter alia*] it is He to Whom we ought to be bound as to our unfailing principle; to Whom also our choice should be resolutely directed as to our last end," (S.T. II.II.81.1). The virtue of justice works in tandem with knowledge of God's existence and nature to create a sub-category of itself, the virtue of religion, which disposes one's will to give to God what he is due. On this, the Scholastics are in general agreement:

> And so religion is defined as 'the virtue through which men deliver the worship owed to God as the first principle of all things'. – (Billuart, 540; trans. mine)

From these words a conclusion may be drawn regarding the

nature of what is properly called religion. Assuredly it is a moral virtue, whereby the service due to God as the unfailing principle and final end is delivered, in those matters which pertain specifically to divine worship. – (Zigliara, 367; trans. mine)

Like all virtues, the virtue of religion elicits in one those acts which are immediately and directly concerned with its object and commands others insofar as they are a means to its end (S.T. II.II.81.1). Devotion, or the will to readily do what pertains to the worship and service of God (S.T. II.II.82.2), and prayer, or the confession of one that God is the "Author of his goods" and petition for those goods (S.T. II.II.83.3), are the principal internal acts elicited by the virtue of religion. These internal acts in turn elicit and command a number of external acts of religion such as bodily reverence, vows or oaths, and sacrifices.

Aristotle says in the Nichomachean Ethics that "the greatest external good we should assume to be what we render to the Gods" and that this is "honor," (NE viii 3.1123b26-28). Just as every virtue is opposed by vice, the virtue of religion is opposed by the vices of superstition and irreligion. Superstition and irreligion are a form of injustice because they deprive the divine of what she is due. Superstition "is a vice contrary to religion by excess, not that it offers more to the divine worship than true religion, but because it offers divine worship either to whom it ought not, or in a manner it ought not," (S.T. II.II.92.1). Irreligion is a vice contrary to religion by way of deficiency because it involves a privation of worship that ought to occur, consisting in a positive irreverence to the divine or in acts which are contrary to the worship that the divine is rightfully due.

As the virtue of religion unfolds in the hearts and minds of people, they may tend toward one another and form a *cultus dei* or *deorum* in which individuals try and relate to the divine as they ought to. Possessed of this virtue, they may exercise in chorus those acts which the virtue of religion elicits and encourage each other to avoid the vices of superstition and irreligion. In other words, the fostering of individual virtue may lead to religious *community*.

But what good does it do to form such a habit or community when the Gods do not need anything from us and there is nothing we could offer them that is not already theirs? As Thomas notes:

> Since justice implies equality, and since we cannot offer God an equal return, it follows that we cannot make Him a perfectly just repayment. For this reason the Divine law is not properly called *jus* but *fas*, because, to wit, God is satisfied if we accomplish what we can. Nevertheless, justice tends to make man repay God as much as he can, by subjecting his mind to Him entirely, (S.T. II.II.57.1).

Aristotle similarly says:

> This, then, is the way in which unequals should associate. The person who is benefited with money or virtue ought to give honour in return, giving back what he can. For friendship seeks what can be done, not what accords with merit, because that is not possible in every case, such as honour to the gods or one's parents. No one could ever make a return corresponding to their worth, but the person who serves them as best he can is thought to be good. (*NE* viii 14.1163b 15-21).

One could also suggest that insofar as 'ought' implies 'can', it is not the case that we ought to repay the Gods what we cannot give – viz. an equal return. Having outlined Aquinas' understanding of the virtue of justice in general as well as of the virtue of religion in particular, we may now attempt to answer the question that we began with: what does it mean for us that the world is constituted by a plurality of polycentric henads?

Consider that in being divinely constituted, we owe the Gods for our very lives: we depend on them not only to exist at all but even to exist from one moment to the next. As we saw in section 3.1 with respect to all things, it is not the case that the Gods ground reality in an initial stage and then withdraw so as to leave the machine to run on its own: there could be nothing around to do anything if the Gods were not there providing the ground for it to be itself at every moment in which it is. There is no inertia in things whereby they persevere as themselves unless and until they are interrupted from doing so: they need, at every single moment, to be divinely constituted because that *just is* part of what it is to be themselves in the first place. As such, we are in a position of *radical* dependence whereby we are so utterly helpless before the Gods that we could not even have the identity of being ourselves without them. Yet our powerlessness to even remain in being for a moment on our own is not just met with abiding constancy but an overflow of good things wherein the Gods author all of our goods and constitute everything that make our lives worth living, such as happiness, adventure, success, companionship and love. Are such things not worth being thankful for? Are those who gift them to us not worthy of acclaim, or to be held in high esteem? Who but the most entitled could be showered with unmerited gifts and feel no need to respond accordingly? I would sooner think it that we should marvel at the Gods.

Our lives are utterly theirs to give and take; a gift that none of us could merit prior to receiving it. Surely there is *some* commonsensical and substantial sense in which it is good of us to be grateful to them and humble before them. Moreover, this gratitude and humility should not be rare or occasional, because neither is their holding us in being here and there: it should be regular or habitual. And because this is something that can be known through reason, it is something we can attain through disciplined effort. But all this is just to say that we ought to be religious in the classical sense expanded on by Aquinas: we *should* thank the Gods and be mindful of our radical dependence upon them. It is a good and wholesome thing to do, it is how we ought to relate to the Gods. And this extends as well to what this virtue inclines us toward as means to its end, such as devotion and prayer.

All this leads to a final consideration on account of which there is a proper way for us to relate to the Gods, and that is the Gods' intrinsic venerability. We should *recognize* or *acknowledge* that simply because of who they are, aside from what they do for us, Gods are truly something to marvel at and be in awe of: they are the most resplendent individuals, as wholly transcendent of everything as they are immersed in the fabric of its very being, uniquely comprehending within themselves everything that is extraordinary and praiseworthy. Plato said that "each God is the most beautiful and best thing possible" (Rep. 381c) and Proclus that "the Gods are the most ancient and venerable of all things" (In Tim. 306, bk. II). Aquinas expands that:

> Reverence is due to God on account of His excellence, which is communicated to certain creatures not in equal measure, but according to a measure of proportion; and so the reverence which we pay to God, and which belongs to latria, differs from the reverence which we pay to certain excellent creatures; this belongs to dulia..." (S.T. II.II.84.1).

One might find the foregoing troubling inasmuch as philosophy only allows us to speak of Gods in collective singulars so that the specific deities one ought to relate to religiously cannot be determined through philosophy. What then are we doing in this chapter? Recommending some centralized religion for all polytheists? Not even remotely. We are not *in any way* recommending some general religion or general religious practice for all polytheists. Rather we are describing in general terms what functions as the heart of particular religions and religious practices.

In a similar vein, one may be concerned about which God we are suggesting the virtue of religion should direct one to. As the polytheist's will deepens in its disposition to render what is due to the Gods, she will incline toward prayer, sacrifice, adoration and devotion. But, is it not impractical to pray and sacrifice to and adore and worship *all* of the Gods? Recall first Aquinas' reply to the concern that one cannot give back perfectly what is owed to God: justice tends to make people repay as much as they can. On this account, one may be tempted to say that justice asks of us that we give what we can to all the Gods through a general devotion, prayer or sacrifice (a generalized justice that Aquinas might count as "distributive justice"; S.T. II.II.61.1). Such a broad practice could be compatible with and respectful of one's more vested relationships with particular deities (relationships Aquinas could say are governed by "commutative justice", *ibid*.). But, in a world that is divinely constituted by a plurality of polycentric henads, each God is, *qua* herself, *all things* so that each God is "the one" to whom the virtue of religion directs us to do right by. In other words, it is not the case that we ought to worship all the Gods in order to do right by any of them or that we ought to worship any one of them in order to do right by all of them. After all, each God is her own way of being all the Gods. Accordingly, far from inclining every polytheist toward some single, uniform religion with the same core practices, polycentricity allows for and encourages the virtue of religion to be expressed multifariously, through solitary, local or regional cults, each with its own Gods who are *more* than qualified to be "the one" to whom justice directs us.

We have found that humans should relate religiously to the Gods. But we have not gone into great detail about how we should worship them, pray to them or offer sacrifices and the like. On the one hand, this is because such matters are to be determined theologically and not philosophically. But, on the other hand, it is because the general project of this work prevents us from going much further than giving the reader a general feel for how it might all work. In this latter respect, it is more important for our purposes to establish *that* we ought to pray than it is *how* we ought to pray. However, the Platonists left behind a rich tradition and understanding of religious acts such as prayer and sacrifice called theurgy (or God-work), as can be found in Iamblichus' *De Mysteriis*, and it cannot be recommended enough to at least give them a chance.

In drawing this chapter to a close, we have but one final task: to allow the inner logic of theism to speak to these matters for itself according to the *a priori* method we have relied on so far throughout this work. Up until this point in this chapter, we have employed a bottom-up approach which takes a certain commonsensical notion of goodness and justice for granted and argues from this to conclusions about the Gods. But, this sort of approach is not really all that in keeping with the general methodology of this work, and so we shall have need to find the foregoing ultimately unsatisfying, at least in the respect of it leaving us with an expectation or curiosity about there being deeper results attainable through a process of reasoning from the Gods rather than to them. As such, we shall turn in these closing remarks once more and for the final time to our characteristic style of reasoning.

Consider then that the idea according to which everything unfolds from each God contains within itself a notion of directionality. That is, it is not just that all things unfold *from* each God, but that they also unfold *toward* some end or result. The procession of being is a procession *from* one point *to* another. Each level of stratification in a God anticipates the next, such that subject as such anticipates predicate as such; which anticipates predication of someone or other; which anticipates predication of someone in particular and so on and so forth. The end result toward which a process unfolds provides the process with its identity such that it is what the process is a process *of*. To illustrate, consider that the conversion of light energy into chemical energy is not an ending result which photosynthesis just keeps accidentally bringing about, but rather it is the very thing that photosynthesis is the process *of*. Similarly, the end of each thing's procession from the Gods is not just some accidental result of divine constitution: it is the very naturally occurring *point* of it. In this way, the end toward which being proceeds provides being with its deepest sense of purpose.

But this end can be none other than the Gods, for they divinely constitute all things, to include the end toward which all things proceed. As such, each God is not only what all things proceed *from*; and so, the originating principle of all things, but also what all things proceed *toward*, and so the final end of all things. The Gods then provide each thing with its deepest sense of purpose; constituting the reason for why it exists at all. Consequently, our deepest purpose in life is to return to the Gods from whom we proceed, attaining them as an end in the way appropriate to who and what we are. Inasmuch as religion is just another name for the means to this end, religion is more than just the right thing for us to do.

Conclusion and Summary

The purpose of this final chapter is to express to the reader what seems to be the most important consequence for mankind of a world that is divinely constituted by a plurality of polycentric henads, and that is that we owe it to the Gods to *respond* to them for all that they are and all that they do. We *should* respond to their splendor and richness in a way that classical thinkers would call *religious*. That is, it is something that we truly ought to do for the Gods to be thankful to them, humble before them, mindful of them and so forth, if not simply because the Gods are intrinsically deserving of this then because they are our ever-present, unfailing principles of life and goodness. But, in doing this, we also pursue fulfillment of our deepest purpose in life.

We began in section 4.1 with a brief and straightforward presentation of a classical understanding of what the virtue of justice is, a view according to which it is a disposition of one to relate to others as she ought to. Because we can come to understand that we ought to relate to others and how we should do so through our reason, the virtue of justice is something that we can attain with disciplined effort. We moved on in section 4.2 by applying this general understanding to the more particular case of how we ought to relate to the Gods. Based on the sheer gravity of how dependent we are on the Gods and the fact that they not only meet us in our radical vulnerability but far and away exceed our needs despite our having no grounds to deserve any of it, the good and decent thing for us to do is to acknowledge them and show some gratitude and humility. But we also found that the concept of procession involves the transition from one point to another, such that the procession of being must be proceeding toward an ending result. Because the Gods constitute all things, they constitute this end as well, and so are themselves the very *point* of each thing's procession, providing everything with its deepest reason for existing.

Of all the consequences for mankind that a world constituted by a plurality of polycentric henads bears, why is the duty to be religious most important? Surely, the Platonists drew other philosophical consequences that were important as well, such as our immortality or even the doctrine of reincarnation? But, while these and other ideas are interesting and can be important for us to know and understand, they do not directly touch upon what we *ought to do*. Moreover, in drawing close to the Gods through such things as prayer, one nurtures a relationship with another in whom all the answers lie. That is to say, relating to the Gods as we ought to can furnish one with a deep and abiding sense of mystery and truth that is far greater than what any book could ever convey. As Iamblichus said:

...the first degree of prayer is the introductory, which leads to contact and acquaintance with the divine; the second is conjunctive, producing a union of sympathetic minds, and calling forth benefactions sent down by the gods even before we express our requests, while achieving whole courses of action even before we think of them; the most perfect, finally, has as its mark ineffable unification, which established all authority in the gods, and provides that our souls rest completely in them. (De Mysteriis, 275)

Closing Remarks

In drawing this work to a close, it is my hope that the reader has developed a feel for the spirit of polytheism and a general idea of how it might all work. It was said at the outset that we would try to answer two basic questions: what does theism amount to, and what do things look like in the bigger picture from the theist's perspective? In answer to the first question, we found that theism amounts to a rich and substantive position about what transcends Nature: a plurality of polycentric henads. But in the very fact of being so completely and utterly themselves; that is, in being henadic, each God is a way of being all things, such that if one looks at everything in the bigger picture, she sees that the encompassing expanse of Nature is from edifice to ledge an integrated, systematic whole; subsisting and enduring in and through finite and divided modes of being that are but their own ways of expressing those who are infinite and undivided. Such is a Platonic approach to theism.

Aristotle said that it was a divinely inspired "tradition handed down from the ancients of the earliest times" that the Gods, who encompass "the whole of nature" are "the primary substances," (Metaphysics 1074b1-10). I hope to have shown some honor to this most ancient of traditions by expressing in new ways these two grand maxims, namely, that the Gods encompass the whole of nature (divine constitution) and that they are the primary substances (henads).

Appendix A

The Argument from Totality

The primary task of the preceding chapters was to come to an understanding of what theism amounts to and bring into focus an image of what everything looks like according to theism. Allowing it to unravel according to its own inner logic, we arrived at a grand metanarrative according to which all things are divinely constituted by a plurality of polycentric henads. But readers might be unsatisfied to just *see* the big picture and not any reasons to believe that it is true. For those who would like to see arguments on its behalf, I offer these appendixes. Each appendix will contain an argument in support of some part of the polytheist picture painted throughout the preceding chapters.

This first appendix will provide an argument that all things are divinely constituted by a plurality of polycentric henads. We shall begin with some preliminary remarks on the argument itself and move on to discuss each premise.

1. Like all pluralities, the totality of all things is either monocentric or polycentric.
2. If it is monocentric, then something is outside the totality of all things.
3. If it is polycentric, then all things are divinely constituted by a multitude of Gods.
4. But nothing is outside the totality of all things.
5. So, all things are divinely constituted by a multitude of Gods.

This argument is presented in a syllogistic format although it is worded slightly informally. It is logically valid, which means that if the premises are true, then so is its conclusion. The most important thing for the reader to discern, then, is whether she believes each premise to be true. There are four premises: (1), (2), (3) and (4) respectively. The remainder of this appendix will unpack and offer considerations on behalf of each premise. In every case, we shall find that the proposition rings with verisimilitude.

1. Like all pluralities, the totality of all things is either monocentric or polycentric.

By 'plurality' we shall mean that which is formed when several or more individuals have something in common. If what they have in common adds to 'who' each member is, such as in the case of their having a property, feature or characteristic in common, then it is a modification of the members in the plurality and not itself a member too. This sort of plurality is called 'monocentric' because the center of its unity is the one, specific thing its members have in common. If, on the other hand, what they have in common does *not* add to 'who' they are, such as in the case of their *having* something in common by *being* it, *albeit* in each their own way, then it is *not* a modification of the members in the plurality and so *is* itself a member of the plurality. This sort of plurality is called 'polycentric' because the center of its unity is any of the many things its members have in common.

2. If it is monocentric, then something is outside the totality of all things.

In light of what has been said so far, it is clear that if the totality of all things is a monocentric plurality, then all things form a plurality because its members each have one, specific thing in common. Whatever that thing is, it is a modification of the members in this plurality and so not itself a member too. But, in this case, something is outside the totality of all things.

3. If it is polycentric, then all things are divinely constituted by

a multitude of Gods.

On the other hand, if the totality of all things is a polycentric plurality; then, in accord with what it is *to be* polycentric, there is a multitude of henads who divinely constitute all things. But, while this might show that there are henads, what does it mean for everything else? After all, how could all things be polycentric if they are not themselves henads? Consider that if a henad is a way of being all things then to be constituted by a henad is for one to be constituted by all things. But, *her* way of being constituted by all things will be in accord with who or what she is, and so mediated – unlike the henads – by the limitations with which she comes. As Proclus says "[a]ll things are in all things, but in each according to its proper nature" (Prop. 103).

4. But nothing is outside the totality of all things.

There must be a totality of all things in order for there to be something *outside* of the totality of all things. But, if there *is* a totality of all things, then nothing is outside of this totality. Indeed, if anything is excluded from the relevant totality, then it is only the totality of all things up to the point of the thing which is outside of it and not the totality of *all* things.

Conclusion

It follows from (2) and (4) by modus tollens that the totality of all things is not monocentric, and from this result and (1) by disjunction that the totality of all things is polycentric. It then follows from (3) by modus ponens that all things are divinely constituted by a plurality of polycentric henads. We have reasoned our way to a crucial thesis, if not *the* crucial thesis of this work, but I cannot pretend to have anticipated every objection or concern. Perhaps certain terms are ambiguous or certain issues have gone unaddressed. In fact, it would be surprising if nothing could be said in disagreement. However, the preceding should, I hope, suffice to provide the reader with an interesting and thought-provoking reason to believe that all things are divinely constituted by a plurality of polycentric henads.

Appendix B

Objections to Polytheism

The purpose of this next appendix is to field various objections to polytheism. Our concern here is not to be exhaustive, but rather to illustrate how little relevance typical objections to polytheism actually bear. Rather than organize the objections chronologically, so that those which come from a more classical mindset will be considered before those which may be considered more analytic, we shall select several representative objections from that period which addressed polytheism directly and with at least some sustained reflection. As we shall see, the formidability of polytheism speaks for itself.

Deep Equivocity

We shall begin by considering some objections from Thomas Aquinas, not only because he represents monotheist objectors with a more classical background in philosophy, but also because he wrote a fair amount about why he disagreed with polytheism, as far as it goes. We shall do just this not so as to rebut objections to polytheism simply for the sake of it, but in the hopes of clarifying the terms of our argument and securing from traditional concerns what we take to have been demonstrated.

The first of only three objections that Aquinas raises to polytheism in his section on the unity of God in S.T. I.11.3 is as follows:

> For it is manifest that the reason why any singular thing is *this particular thing* is because it cannot be communicated to many: since that whereby Socrates is a man, can be communicated to many; whereas, what makes him this particular man, is

only communicable to one. Therefore, if Socrates were a man by what makes him to be this particular man, as there cannot be many Socrates, so there could not in that way be many men. Now this belongs to God alone; for God Himself is His own nature, as was shown above (Q. 3, A. 3). Therefore, in the very same way God is God, and He is this God. Impossible is it therefore that many Gods should exist.

The idea here is that because of God's utter simplicity, what makes God to be divine is also what makes God to be this God in particular. As such, the same thing that would make each in a plurality of Gods to be divine would also make them each to be only one God in particular. By this argument, polytheism is more of a confusion than a mere falsehood: it fails to grasp something fundamental about God's utter simplicity.

This is a rare example in which a monotheist thinker has approached polycentricity in close conceptual proximity. Aquinas is not wrong that each in a plurality of Gods will have divinity in common. Nor is he wrong that, in our words, divinity is not a monad but a henad. But where he errs is in thinking that it must be some privileged henad in particular and not just any henad as such. This is not only assumed without argument, but contrary to the notion of henadicity itself, whereby one is *too* simple to be the only one of anything. By contradictorily placing a henad in a category so as to be the only one of something, Aquinas unwittingly naturalizes the divine and advocates a form of atheism.

Aquinas privileges a henad elsewhere in his objections to polytheism. For example, in *De Ente et Essentia* n. 78, he argues that there can be only one thing in which there is no difference between essence and existence because there are only three ways to plurify a thing, and being itself transcends all of them (Bobik 1965, 160). In other words, Aquinas is assuming that a multitude of Gods would be a plurification of this one thing, being itself.

Commenting on these passages, Joseph Bobik argues:

> To the possible objection that St. Thomas has not shown that the three ways of multiplying exhaust all possibilities, this is to be said. Whatever be the number of ways which one might be able to devise for multiplying something, if *what is being multiplied* is to be found among the members of the resulting plurality, it must be taken in a pure or unmixed state; this is why it can never be more than one. All other members of the plurality must be taken with some addition; otherwise they will not be distinguishable from each other or from *what is being plurified,* (Bobik 1965, 171).

In rather explicit terms then, divinity is being identified with one henad in particular, so as to claim that one could not be divine without being that particular henad. But of course, such an assumption merely begs the question and, in any case, yields a deeply confused position.

It should be argued that a plurality of Gods could not have any property, feature or characteristic in common with one another, let alone a divine nature, because there is nothing more to a God than herself. It is in this respect that each deity is "henadic", for she is a "henad" who is irreducibly individual. But if one does not take into consideration that the only thing which henads could have in common is each other, then she may be liable to think the henads could not have anything in common *at all*, and this raises another objection to polytheism.

If the Gods do not have any properties, features or characteristics in common, there may not appear to be any way to refer to more than one God without using the same term to mean completely different things, thereby equivocating. Indeed, Aquinas seemed to be aware of this issue, and he dismisses as equivocal any polytheism on which the Gods do not have a divine nature in common. Traditionally attributed to Thomas

Aquinas, the *Compendium Theologiae*, Chapter 15 says:

> If there were many gods, they would be called by this name
> either equivocally or univocally. If they are called gods
> equivocally, further discussion is fruitless; there is nothing to
> prevent other peoples from applying the name "god" to what
> we call a stone. If they are called gods univocally, they must
> agree either in genus or in species. But we have just shown
> that God can be neither a genus nor a species comprising
> many individuals under Himself. Accordingly a multiplicity
> of gods is impossible, (1947, 41).

Reiterating this dismissal in *Summa Contra Gentiles* (S.C.G.)
I.42.12, Thomas says:

> ...if there are two gods, either the name *God* is predicated of
> both univocally, or equivocally. If equivocally, this is outside
> our present purpose. Nothing prevents any given thing from
> being equivocally named by any given name, provided we
> admit the usage of those who express the name, (1975, 42.12).

Aquinas' dismissive attitude might strike one as inappropriate
or unwarranted because it may not seem that just *anything* could
fairly be called "God": it must transcend Nature, one might say,
for example. But, if the Gods do not have anything in common,
they do not have "transcending Nature" in common either, at
least insofar as it is a 'what' in its own right which they plurify
or multiply realize. The charge of equivocation may thus seem
graver than initial appearances: plural references in our domain
of theological discourse will equivocate pervasively and all the
way down, such that at no point will plural terms communicate
anything meaningful. Any attempt to disambiguate the
references will either collapse into grammatical singularity or
equivocate once again and on to infinity. We shall call this the

problem of deep equivocity, and it may be thought to show that polytheistic theological discourse is unintelligible.

But this whole way of objecting to polytheism is deeply misguided. It is not the case that if the Gods cannot have any 'what' in common, then they cannot have anything in common. Indeed, the only thing they could have in common is each other. As such, only one who is polycentric may be called God in a strict sense. In this way, we may say that not just *anything* can be called a God.

Aquinas admits in S.T. I.3.3 that "[w]e can speak of simple things only as though they were like the composite things from which we derive our knowledge." And the grammatical plurality within our domain of theological discourse is indeed like the grammatical plurality within our domains of non-theological discourse, specifically in that it functions to predicate or attribute something of many. However, it differs therefrom at least insofar as it does not thereby assume that what the many have in common is some 'what'. This difference is only to be expected when it is kept in mind that the grammatical plurality within our domains of non-theological discourse serves to capture the structure of plurality among beings, a structure whereby individuals form a plurality by each being the same type of thing. For this reason, such grammatical plurality cannot capture the structure of plurality among the Gods and can be applied to them only at the cost of falling into categorical error: the Gods belong to a group that is not itself a type of thing. As Edward Butler says in his dissertation:

> The One is truly and fully manifest in each of the henads, each of which can as such serve as the center in a system which would therefore posit the others on its periphery – hence 'polycentricity.' At the same time, there can be no *unique* center, for this would totalize and, as it were, *crystallize* the entire field "for another," and the individuality of the henads

transcends mediated unity or unity "for another". (Butler 2003, 59).

The only problem that deep equivocity raises is for its characterization of polytheism.

Divine Inseparability

Proclus says that Gods "transcend all relation," (Prop. 126). But, as we shall see, there is another kind of objection that Aquinas brings against polytheism – not only as the final of his principal concerns in S.T. I.11.3, but several times in S.C.G. 1.42 as well – which takes it for granted that Gods would have relations and focuses on how a plurality of Gods could *operate* together. This sort of objection is regularly given in monotheist sources. For Aquinas, if there were many Gods, then there are in reality several things that should not be, including a sort of unity he saw in the world and the causation he believed it to require on the part of God. We have chosen to interact with this kind of objection despite its reliance on the mistaken assumptions that polytheism would involve a monocentric plurification, let alone of being itself, still less that the Gods would cause things rather than constitute them, because it provides an opportunity to clarify the inseparability of the Gods which is implicit in polycentricity. Rather than discuss the details specific to these objections, which would require us to examine a number of complicated metaphysical subjects, we shall address them in a general way by developing the divine inseparability of the Gods.

Consider that as subject *qua* subject, each God precedes all relations to anything else: there is only their perspective in this position and so no complexifying predicates under consideration for them to relate to. *Qua* themselves, they are each, as it were, in a state of absolute precedence. But, being separate from one another is a relation. As such, separation must be among those relations which the Gods precede. The separation relation obtains in a variety of contexts: objects can be spatially separate, events can be temporally separate, spouses can be maritally separated, and concepts can be categorically separate and so forth. The Gods precede the separation relation as such and thus regardless of context: they are not separated by power or pedigree, nor are they entitatively separated beings. This result may strike one as reducing polytheism to monotheism. Indeed, if the Gods each exist in a state of absolute precedence, it may seem that the reason they cannot be related to one another is that it is true for each that there is no other God for them to be related to. However, the Gods do not precede *one another*, they precede *relation* to one another. As such, what is true for each God in the state of absolute precedence is that she is related to nothing, not that there is nothing for her to be related to. When we say that the Gods are inseparable, it is not because it is true for each God in the state of absolute precedence that there are no Gods for her to be separate from, but because nothing separates the Gods from one another.

Interestingly, a result of this divine inseparability is that any reference to one God just is a reference to all the Gods, *albeit* not to all the Gods *qua* all the Gods. Moreover, granting that the Gods have knowledge, there is no mystery in whether the Gods could know of one another in light of their non-relationality, for they are epistemically inseparable, such that for one God to know herself just is for her to know all the Gods, *albeit* not to know all the Gods *qua* all the Gods.

Still, their transcendence of the separation relation may give one the impression that the Gods are in reality just the same God; but, while they are inseparable, they are not identical. One might protest that to be non-identical just is to be separate in some sense, but the individuality of the Gods is not relational and so does not consist in their being distinct from one another: it is not negative, implying their identity by negating all that they are not, but something positive. Theirs is individuation, not differentiation.

Moreover, just because the Gods are inseparable does not mean that the Gods are inseparably *united* – at least without qualification. After all, unitive relations are relations, and are for that reason among those things which the Gods *qua* themselves precede. As such, the Gods are not inseparably united into a group, a sort of entity or anything else for that matter.

Although the Gods do transcend unitive relations, nevertheless each God is "in" all of the Gods and all of the Gods are "in" each God, not as parts of a whole or as stuff that is contained, but simply as individuals between which there is no separation of any kind. To refer to one God then is indeed to refer to all of the Gods, but only to all of the Gods insofar as they are inseparable from that one God. Likewise, if a God knows herself, she thereby knows all of the Gods, but only as they are inseparable from herself.

In light of the foregoing, we may say that the Gods do not *operate* as separate individuals, converging upon a single effect or discretely governing portions of reality. Their acts of will – granting we may attribute "will" to the Gods – are inseparable. Nor for that matter could the Gods' non-identical wills be in dissonance with one another, for quarrel and disagreement are just more relations the Gods precede. In general, if the Gods could not operate together under a relation, it is not because the Gods could not operate together at all, but because they do not stand in that relation to begin with.

The foregoing may give the impression that because the Gods could not disagree, they therefore could only ever will the same thing. But as we saw in Section 2.2, a God is qua herself the thing which all the other Gods have in common. Zeus, for example, is qua himself in all the other Gods as Zeuseity. In this position, Zeus is all-encompassing. Insofar as the other Gods are in Zeus, Zeus' will is enacted *through* their wills, as they are, in this position, *zeuseical* like all things. Likewise, Odin is qua himself what all the other Gods have in common, including Zeus from our previous example. He is in them *as* Odinity, and their wills are *odinic*, like everything else. It is in *this* position, of a God qua herself, that each God precedes relation and is therefore inseparable from all those within her. It is not as if each God is in this position at the same time, and lined up side by side, capable of willing in unison or in dissonance: the Gods are only ever either in another God, or the one in whom the other Gods are. *Qua* in another God, the Gods may will divergently because they are not, in this position, preceding of all things, relation included.

Appendix C

On the Necessity of Nature

The purpose of this final appendix is to examine a reason for thinking that Nature exists out of necessity. The idea here is not that there is some one specific part of Nature that exists in every possible world, such as an initial state or a privileged particle, but that in every possible world there is that in anything which makes it to be natural. The reason why this element of the book is considered important enough to devote an appendix to is that monotheism is so often motivated by arguments to the effect that Nature requires a cause. The constitutive model of polytheism stands in sharp contrast to all such causal models, as deeply ingrained as they have become for the field's dialectic, and so it is an important part of the Platonic system to motivate. As we saw in Chapter 3, the necessity of Nature is *predicted* by the emanationist so that it is part of what it all looks like in the big picture from the theist's perspective and marks a crucial part in the system we presented. The argument here will begin by developing a preliminary understanding of the 'being' that Nature comes in different forms of and argue that the denial of such a thing's existence is more severe than merely unlikely on balance, less theoretically beneficial than its alternative or even downright false: it is absurd.

What is being?

In common parlance, the term "existence" refers to what is *real*. In this sense, for one to exist is for her to not be illusory or made up. This is a looser or at least less precise notion of existence than what we shall have in mind. As we said in section 1.2, there is a sense of existence in which it is itself a 'what'; indeed, the most general of all 'whats', because every single thing that exists, no matter how different, has it in common at the very least that it is *some* type of thing or other. Existence is thus not *a* type but what makes types *to be* types, it is what they all have in common. In this sense, there *are* many things, and one can propose as categories of being everything from objects and properties to relations and events: all such things are types.

Beings come in different forms, have distinct features or properties and subsist within an exemplification nexus: they are limited, determinate, qualified and differentiated. However, "being" is what makes things to be, it is not what makes them to be this or that sort of thing. For example, while quarks exist, what it is for x to be a quark is not that x *exists*. As such, existence is not that in virtue of which a quark is a quark, it is that in virtue of which a quark exists. In other words, it is by being the type of thing that quarks are that something is a quark, but it is by being an instance of any type of thing at all that a thing *exists*.

As such, if we consider any type at all precisely insofar as it is a type, we discover a 'what' and the most general of all 'whats' at that: what-ness itself. It is not this or that existing thing, but existence itself. What is the status of this 'what'? Is there *really* such a thing? That is, is there such a *thing* as existence? At first pass, the question may strike one as smacking of reification: while all beings have it in common that they exist, surely existence does not *itself* exist. But while existence *as it is held* in common between all beings may not strike one as a thing in its own right; what of this existence when it is considered in and of itself? What *is it* that all beings have in common? What *is* being itself?

We argued in section 1.2 that one can only be a type of thing if *she* is around in the first place: the property of being a type of thing is something that is attributed to a subject; which implies that the subject *qua* subject, or the individual considered independent of being any type of thing, is *there* and so established with *some* sense of reality on her own, lest no one be around to bear the property of being a type of thing. As such, the very idea that one is a type of thing presupposes that there is more to her than just herself: there is, in addition, the type of thing that *she* is. In other words, there is a distinction in things between themselves and 'what' they are. But there can be no such distinction in what is simply being itself: existence does not add anything to being itself; it is no type of thing, and so there is nothing more to it than itself; it *is* existence. As such, it is what is present in every category of being – concrete or abstract – the clay out of which all things are formed, the form of which all other forms partake. Such a thing would not exemplify or instantiate any properties or features nor would it be limited or qualified by any form or category of being which are all subsequent to being itself. In fact, existence *is* limitation, inasmuch as what types of things do is limit or qualify one to be such-and-such.

The Existence of Existence

The argument of this appendix is not only that there is no cogent way to deny the existence of being itself, but that there is no way to cogently suspend judgment on the matter either. To understand the proposed difficulties, we must first look into what the existential negation involves.

Like all propositions, negations are comprised of a subject and a predicate. But, unlike other negations, the existential negation denies existence rather than truth, and therefore only distributes *de re* and not *de dicto*. As such, the existential negation must deny some predicate of a subject. Moreover, its operation can range over individuals as well as objects of a higher order, such as sets, kinds, or concepts. By virtue of being existential, a negation must deny of a subject some predicate that is related to existence; but what that is will depend on whether the subject is an individual or an object of a higher order. While first-order existential negations directly deny that an individual exists, higher-order existential negations deny that something of a higher order than an individual is satisfied, instantiated or even supervened upon. We shall contend that neither first nor higher order existential negations can cogently apply to being itself.

To begin, consider that nothing which is being itself could satisfy, instantiate or supervene upon anything; not because being itself is impossible, but because whatever could satisfy, instantiate or supervene upon anything is such that it could have something other than its own existence as a principle of identity or intelligibility, and this is not true of being itself. As such, higher-order existential negations of being itself will be in categorical error. Indeed, for the same reason, higher-order existential *affirmations* of being itself will be in categorical error. It follows that being itself can only cogently be affirmed or negated in a first-order way.

The problem here is that for many the first-order existential negation seems contradictory: it commits to an individual's existence by referring to that individual but then, in the same breath, it reneges on that commitment by negating that individual's existence. On this account, there can be no cogent first-order existential negation of being itself – or indeed of anything for that matter. However, perhaps one is committed to an understanding of "individuals" that removes existential import from first-order references to individuals. Perhaps one will say that first-order references to individuals are really just references to the individuals themselves and not to the individuals insofar as they are this or that type of thing. Or perhaps one will say that first-order references to individuals are really just references to individuals insofar as they are conceivably of this or that type rather than insofar as they truthfully are.

But however, one wishes to cash the idea out, what can be referred to in a first-order way without any existential commitment must in some way be distinct from 'what' it is, and there can be no such distinction for being itself. So, if we refer to being itself in a first-order way, we either do so with or without existential commitment, and in either case, there is no cogent way to deny its existence. Given that the only way to deny the existence of being itself is in a first-order way or in a higher-order way, it turns out that there is no cogent way to deny its existence.

Some may think this has all been too fast. Perhaps there is a way to speak about propositions concerning being itself rather than about being itself directly. However, if these propositions are to be existential, they must treat of being itself and they can only do this in either a first or higher-order way: as was indicated above, existential negations distribute *de re*, not *de dicto*. Otherwise, they are not negating something existential, but something alethic.

For all that has been said thus far, it does not follow that it is *absurd* to deny the existence of being itself; only that it is not cogent to do so, and so one might think that while reason forbids denying the existence of being itself, it permits agnosticism about whether there is being itself. To understand why existential negations of being itself are absurd, we must call to mind that subset of negations which concern denying of something at least part of what it is to be that something. For example, part of what it is for x to be water is that x is H2O. Thus, the negation "water is not H2O" belongs to this subset. Similarly, to be in molecular motion is what it is to have heat. As such, the negation "fire is not in molecular motion" belongs to this subset as well. But, consider that neither of the two preceding examples involve existential negations, and this is because for a negation in this subset to be *existential*, it must deny the existence of that x for which existence is at least part of what it is to be x.

As we have argued thus far, "being itself" just is its own existence. For this reason, to say that being itself does not exist is more like saying that water is not H20, or that fire is not in molecular motion than it is like saying George Washington was elected president in 1790 instead of 1789: false; yes, but also deeply confused. It is from the deep misunderstanding involved in denying the existence of being itself that we may regard such negations as "absurd."

To further illustrate the point, it may even be an injustice to say that Nature exists "necessarily" because necessary existence is weaker than the existence of being itself. Consider that while "necessary existence" does indicate that one could not fail to exist, it does not indicate why this is the case, and is thus entirely compatible with it being because one has a principle of existence out of an inexplicable necessity or as the result of some necessary causal activity or event. By contrast, "self-existence" does indicate why being itself could not fail to exist, and that is because existence is not something which being itself has or does, but something that it is. Note that while the aseity of being itself might be utterly incompatible with worldviews on which Nature is *created*, it causes no issues at all with theism, according to which being itself is not *caused* by the Gods but *constituted* by them.

Being itself is not the sort of thing about which one could cogently or without deep confusion wonder whether or not it really exists, as if one would need reason to think that it *has* a principle of existence: it *just is* existence. For this reason, it is an understatement to say that the existence of being itself is necessary, and as we have implied, more appropriate to describe it as *"a se."*

The foregoing argumentation shows that reason does not permit agnosticism toward the subject, for while one may be mistaken but reasonable in suspending judgement on what is necessarily true, one may not suspend judgment on the existence of being itself without deeply misunderstanding that about which one is suspending judgment. As such, reason requires that we affirm in a first-order way that being itself exists, or in other words that there exists that in which there is no difference between identity and existence.

Recommended Reading

Oppy, Graham, *Naturalism and Religion: a Contemporary Philosophical Investigation*. Routledge, an Imprint of the Taylor & Francis Group, 2018.

Butler, Edward: "Damascian Negativity," Dionysius Vol. 37, 2019, pp. 114-133 Ineffability and Unity in Damascius. Butler, Edward. Paper presented at the American Philosophical Association Eastern Division Annual Meeting (Philadelphia, Dec. 28th, 2014). https://henadology.files.wordpress.com/2014/12/ineffability-and-unity-in-damascius.pdf

"The Intelligible Gods in the *Platonic Theology* of Proclus," *Méthexis: International Journal for Ancient Philosophy* Vol. 21, 2008, pp. 131-143.

"The Second Intelligible Triad and the Intelligible-Intellective Gods," *Méthexis: International Journal for Ancient Philosophy* Vol. 23, 2010, pp. 137-157.

"The Third Intelligible Triad and the Intellective Gods," *Méthexis: International Journal for Ancient Philosophy* Vol. 25, 2012, pp. 131-150.

"The Intelligible Gods in the *Platonic Theology* of Proclus," *Méthexis: International Journal for Ancient Philosophy* Vol. 21, 2008, pp. 131-143.

Saffrey, H.D., and Westerink, L. G., 1968–1997, *Proclus: Théologie platonicienne*, 6 vol., (Series: Collection des Universités de France), Paris: Les Belles Lettres.

Steel, Carlos, and Jan Opsomer, translators. *Proclus: On the Existence of Evils*. Edited by Richard Sorabji, Bloomsbury Publishing plc 2014.

Shaw, Gregory, *Theurgy and the Soul the Neoplatonism of Iamblichus*. 2nd ed., Angelico Press, 2014.

Taylor, Thomas, 1816, *Proclus' Theology of Plato*, (Series: The Thomas Taylor Series, VIII), London: Prometheus Trust. [Reprint]

Bibliography

Aristotle:

Metaphysics. Translated by C.D.C. Reeve. Indianapolis, IN: Hacket Publishing Company, 2016.

Nichomachean Ethics. Translated by Roger Crisp. Cambridge, UK: Cambridge University Press, 2000.

Aquinas, Thomas:

Compendium of Theology. Translated by Cyril O. Vollert. St. Louis: B. Herder Book, 1947. Copyright 2012. Veritatis Splendor Publications. Kindle Edition.

Summa Contra Gentiles. Translated by Anton C. Pegis. Notre Dame, IN: University of Notre Dame Press, 1975. Kindle Edition.

Summa Theologiae Prima Pars, 1-49. Translated by Laurence Shapcote. Edited by John Mortensen and Enrique Alarcón. Lander, WY: Aquinas Institute for the Study of Sacred Doctrine, 2012.

Billuart, Charles René, *Summa Sancti Thomae* V4: Hodiernis Academiarum Moribus Accommodata Sive Cursus Theologiae (1904). Vol. IV. N.p.: Kessinger, LLC, 2010.

Bobik, Joseph, and Thomas Aquinas. *Aquinas on Being and Essence: A Translation and Interpretation*. Notre Dame, IN: University of Notre Dame Press, 1965.

Butler, Edward, "The Metaphysics of Polytheism in Proclus," New School for Social Research, New York, 2003.

Cicero, Marcus Tullius, and H. M. Hubbell. *De Inventione; De Optimo Genere Oratorum*; Topica. London: Heinemann, 1949.

D'Hoine, Pieter, et al. "The One, The Henads, and The Principles." All from One: a Guide to Proclus, Oxford: Oxford University Press, 2017.

Iamblichus. *Iamblichus: on The Mysteries*. Translated by John M. Dillon et al., Society of Biblical Literature, 2003.

Oppy, G. R., (2018). *Naturalism and religion: a contemporary philosophical investigation.* Routledge.

Plotinus, Plotinus. *The Enneads.* Edited by Lloyd P. Gerson. Translated by George Boys-Stones et al., Cambridge University Press, 2019.

Proclus:

The Elements of Theology. Ed. and trans. E.R. Dodds. 2nd ed. Oxford: Clarendon Press, 1963.

Commentary on Plato's Timaeus. Book 2: Proclus on the Causes of the Cosmos and Its Creation. Vol. 2. Translated by Runia, David T., and Michael Share, Cambridge University Press, 2008.

Proclus' Commentary on Plato's Parmenides. Translated by Glenn R. Morrow and John M. Dillon, Princeton University Press, 1987.

Suárez, Francisco, *Opera Omnia.* Vol. 13. Parisiis: Vives, 1859.

Zigliara, Tommaso Maria, *Propaedeutica Ad Sacram Theologiam.* 4th ed. Romae: Ex Typ. Polyglotta S.C. De Propaganda Fide, 1903.

MOON
BOOKS

PAGANISM & SHAMANISM

What is Paganism? A religion, a spirituality, an alternative
belief system, nature worship? You can find support for all these
definitions (and many more) in dictionaries, encyclopaedias, and
text books of religion, but subscribe to any one and the truth will
evade you. Above all Paganism is a creative pursuit, an encounter
with reality, an exploration of meaning and an expression of the
soul. Druids, Heathens, Wiccans and others, all contribute their
insights and literary riches to the Pagan tradition. Moon Books
invites you to begin or to deepen your own encounter, right here,
right now.

If you have enjoyed this book, why not tell other readers by
posting a review on your preferred book site.

Recent bestsellers from Moon Books are:

Journey to the Dark Goddess
How to Return to Your Soul
Jane Meredith
Discover the powerful secrets of the Dark Goddess and transform your depression, grief and pain into healing and integration.
Paperback: 978-1-84694-677-6 ebook: 978-1-78099-223-5

Shamanic Reiki
Expanded Ways of Working with Universal Life Force Energy
Llyn Roberts, Robert Levy
Shamanism and Reiki are each powerful ways of healing; together, their power multiplies. *Shamanic Reiki* introduces techniques to help healers and Reiki practitioners tap ancient healing wisdom.
Paperback: 978-1-84694-037-8 ebook: 978-1-84694-650-9

Pagan Portals – The Awen Alone
Walking the Path of the Solitary Druid
Joanna van der Hoeven
An introductory guide for the solitary Druid, *The Awen Alone* will accompany you as you explore, and seek out your own place within the natural world.
Paperback: 978-1-78279-547-6 ebook: 978-1-78279-546-9

A Kitchen Witch's World of Magical Herbs & Plants
Rachel Patterson
A journey into the magical world of herbs and plants, filled with magical uses, folklore, history and practical magic. By popular writer, blogger and kitchen witch, Tansy Firedragon.
Paperback: 978-1-78279-621-3 ebook: 978-1-78279-620-6

Medicine for the Soul
The Complete Book of Shamanic Healing
Ross Heaven
All you will ever need to know about shamanic healing and how to
become your own shaman...
Paperback: 978-1-78099-419-2 ebook: 978-1-78099-420-8

Shaman Pathways – The Druid Shaman
Exploring the Celtic Otherworld
Danu Forest
A practical guide to Celtic shamanism with exercises and
techniques as well as traditional lore for exploring the Celtic
Otherworld.
Paperback: 978-1-78099-615-8 ebook: 978-1-78099-616-5

Traditional Witchcraft for the Woods and Forests
A Witch's Guide to the Woodland with Guided Meditations and
Pathworking
Mélusine Draco
A Witch's guide to walking alone in the woods, with guided
meditations and pathworking.
Paperback: 978-1-84694-803-9 ebook: 978-1-84694-804-6

Wild Earth, Wild Soul
A Manual for an Ecstatic Culture
Bill Pfeiffer
Imagine a nature-based culture so alive and so connected,
spreading like wildfire. This book is the first flame...
Paperback: 978-1-78099-187-0 ebook: 978-1-78099-188-7

Naming the Goddess
Trevor Greenfield
Naming the Goddess is written by over eighty adherents and
scholars of Goddess and Goddess Spirituality.
Paperback: 978-1-78279-476-9 ebook: 978-1-78279-475-2

Shapeshifting into Higher Consciousness
Heal and Transform Yourself and Our World with Ancient
Shamanic and Modern Methods
Llyn Roberts
Ancient and modern methods that you can use every day to
transform yourself and make a positive difference in the world.
Paperback: 978-1-84694-843-5 ebook: 978-1-84694-844-2

Readers of ebooks can buy or view any of these bestsellers by
clicking on the live link in the title. Most titles are published in
paperback and as an ebook. Paperbacks are available in traditional
bookshops. Both print and ebook formats are available online.

Find more titles and sign up to our readers' newsletter at
http://www.johnhuntpublishing.com/paganism
Follow us on Facebook at https://www.facebook.com/MoonBooks
and Twitter at https://twitter.com/MoonBooksJHP